0-8057-7506-4 $21.95

PAUL
THEROUX

Contemporary American writer Paul Theroux
has attracted widespread attention for his best-
selling novel *The Mosquito Coast* and its recent
film adaptation; his travel books, which include
The Great Railway Bazaar and *The Old Patagonian Express*; and his collections of short stories,
including *The Consul's File* and *The London
Embassy*. Theroux, who has lived in England
since 1971, writes about postcolonial life in
Third World countries, exploring the effects of
the world's domination by American culture in
all forms. His work has been widely acclaimed
as marking a movement away from modernist
experimentation and a return to nineteenth-
century realism with Gothic overtones.

Samuel Coale's *Paul Theroux* is the first book-
length study of this acclaimed author. Challenging critics' classification of Theroux as a British
writer, Coale examines Theroux's distinctly
American roots and compares his themes and
techniques with those of nineteenth-century
masters such as Hawthorne and James. He explores Theroux as a romantic realist, suggests
connections between his fiction and travel
works, and uncovers his recurring concerns:
man's inner struggle with fear, his futile attempt
to reshape the world, and the clash of different
cultures. A ground-breaking study, this book is a
much-needed introduction to Theroux, for stu-
dents and fans alike.

Paul Theroux

Twayne's United States Authors Series

Warren French, Editor

University of Swansea, Wales

TUSAS 520

PAUL THEROUX
(1941–   )
Photograph by Jerry Bauer.
Reproduced courtesy of Houghton Mifflin Company.

Paul Theroux

By Samuel Coale

Wheaton College

Twayne Publishers
A Division of G. K. Hall & Co. • *Boston*

Paul Theroux

Samuel Coale

Copyright 1987 by G.K. Hall & Co.
All rights reserved.
Published by Twayne Publishers
A Division of G.K. Hall & Co.
70 Lincoln Street
Boston, Massachusetts 02111

Copyediting supervised by Lewis DeSimone
Book production by Bernadette Montalvo
Book design by Barbara Anderson

Typeset in 11 pt. Garamond
by Modern Graphics, Inc.,
Weymouth, Massachusetts

Printed on permanent/durable acid-free paper
and bound in the United States of America

Library of Congress Cataloging in Publication Data

Coale, Samuel.
  Paul Theroux.

  (Twayne's United States authors series ; TUSAS 520)
  Bibliography: p.
  Includes index.
  1. Theroux, Paul—Criticism and interpretation.
I. Title. II. Series.
PS3570.H4Z6 1987   813′.54   87–2885
ISBN 0–8057–7506–4 (alk. paper)

To Gray and Sam
"Traveling on your own
can be terribly lonely . . ."

Contents

About the Author

Samuel Coale, who has taught American literature at Wheaton College since 1968, is the author of *In Hawthorne's Shadow: American Romance from Melville to Mailer* (Kentucky, 1985), *Anthony Burgess* (Ungar, 1981), and the first full-length critical study of *John Cheever* (Ungar, 1977). He has written extensively on such writers as Frost, Faulkner, Whitman, Kosinski, Coover, Poe, and others. In 1976–77 he was the Fulbright-Hays Senior Lecturer in American literature at Aristotelian University in Thessaloniki, Greece. He has also lectured and taught in Poland, Czechoslovakia, Pakistan, Sweden, and India. He received a National Endowment for the Humanities Fellowship for College Teachers in 1981. He has been chair of the Rhode Island Committee for the Humanities and the Humanities coordinator and moderator for the Public Symposia Program at Trinity Square Repertory Theatre in Providence, Rhode Island, a program which won the first Schwartz Prize in 1981 for the best national Humanities program in the country. He received his Ph.D. in American Civilization in 1970 from Brown University. Currently he lives in Providence with his wife, his son, his dog, and his new word processor.

Preface

In the past several years Paul Theroux has come into his own as a writer, particularly with his novel *The Mosquito Coast,* his travel books, which include *The Great Railway Bazaar* and *The Old Patagonian Express,* and his collections of short stories, which include *The Consul's File* and *The London Embassy.* This is the first full-length critical study of Theroux as man and author at a time when public interest in him has reached a peak.

Theroux has been described by reviewers and critics as a highly polished observer, a realistic writer who can be in his observations both perceptive and pigheaded. What critics have failed to explore, however, is the romantic consciousness within that realistic style and structure and Theroux's double-edged appreciation and denigration of it. The situation has changed since the provincial years prior to World War II; the world is now dominated by American culture in its many forms, and Theroux has surveyed the effects and results of that historical metamorphosis in his fiction and in his travel writing. His explorations of the romantic consciousness both as an extension of and comment upon the spread of American culture provide the often subtle and always intriguing focus of his art. At the same time he does not write in the "post-modernist" manner of many experimental fiction writers, but rather reveals his own roots in traditional storytelling and plot structure.

The aim of this study is twofold, in that it examines both Theroux's American roots and the themes and techniques of his art when seen from an American perspective. So many critics and reviewers have viewed Theroux as a quasi-British writer that it is time to examine him and his work more closely in relation to his very American background.

First of all, critics have defined Theroux as a British writer because he has lived in England since 1971, because his subject matter strikes many readers as particularly British, and because his fertile career as a professional man of letters, rather than as the more typical American writer who infrequently writes "Great Big Novels," strikes many critics as more British than American. He writes about post-colonial life in Third World countries, influenced strongly by such

British writers as Joseph Conrad, Graham Greene, Somerset Maugham, E. M. Forster, and the younger Anthony Burgess, and about the clash between the end of empire and the emergence of new, troubled times. He shares with V. S. Naipaul, a writer whom he admires greatly, a decisively dark view of existence in these places.

Theroux's outlook, however, coincides with that of most serious American fiction. The clash between various cultures is as American as Hawthorne and Henry James. Theroux's attitude toward travel and that of many of the self-deluding visions of his characters share the traditional American faith in self-renewal and rebirth. They partake of the great American myth built upon visions of continued promise and one's ability to reshape the world in one's own image, both partaking of the supposedly limitless reserves of the human imagination and of man's ability to subdue any wilderness, including the darkest one within his own mind.

Theroux's techniques and themes have never been critically examined in any detail before. He is, indeed, a close observer of details fraught with symbolic significance for a culture, a people, or a character. He sets up emblematic encounters in both his fiction and his travel books, seeking in confrontation the often-embattled perspectives of his art. His precise, ironic style mirrors the kind of New England voice recently described by Thomas Williams as "an injunction to use language very carefully, to resist the ordinary consistencies of diction and thought, those automatic responses that obliterate what is darker . . . quite often the Yankee style is an incentive to cruelty." ("New England Voices," *New York Times Book Review*, 19 January 1986, 26). His extremely well crafted and carefully structured plots reveal his commitment to traditional fiction.

Theroux juxtaposes a culture's or a character's illusions and myths with actual facts and incidents, as if decay and disruption were the true state of the world, and any sense of harmony and reconciliation were in some way bound to be suspect. He likes to place an individual self in an alien landscape—himself or his characters—and see which will possess the other. This basic device or vision of conflicting opposites defines the field of Theroux's fiction and travel writing and links his work to other Manichean conflicts in such writers as Hawthorne, Melville, John Gardner, Joyce Carol Oates, William Styron, Robert Coover, and others, however different his techniques. The individual self and the landscape both oppose and define one another, and in his darker tales, the individual consciousness is often locked within itself, "encapsulated" in its own fears and desires. That sense of entrapment, again, links Theroux to the great dark American writers of both the nineteenth and twentieth centuries.

In order to examine carefully Theroux's work, I have divided it up into more or less obvious categories, examining first his life up to the present and the general contours of his art and then looking at his travel books—travel for Theroux strikes me as the impetus of his life and art—his collections of short stories, the early and later novels, and in the final chapter, as through the entire book, the thematic and technical connections between everything he has written.

One of the main strengths of Theroux's later novels is his creation of strong, central characters. In *Waldo* (1967), his first novel, this tendency first appears, as it does later in *Saint Jack* (1973) and again in *The Black House* (1974). However, both the later *The Black House* and *Girls At Play* strike me as decidedly gothic novels, and therefore I have included them in the chapter on the early novels, saving a discussion of *Saint Jack* for the chapter on the later novels. With this exception the novels are discussed, like everything else, in the chronological order of their publication in order to observe Theroux's increasing power and success as a writer.

Paul Theroux has now created a distinctive body of work and is in need of greater critical attention. His perspective is refreshing, in that it broadens the usual American writer's fascination with his own time and place and transcends the often provincial focus of that interest. I hope this first study will lead to a recognition of Theroux's achievements as a writer and to further critical appreciation and exploration of his work.

Samuel Coale

Wheaton College

Acknowledgments

I would like to thank the following for permission to use copyright material: Houghton Mifflin for permission to quote from Paul Theroux's novels, short story collections, and travel books; Hamish Hamilton for permission to quote from the English editions of *Fong and the Indians* and *Sinning with Annie;* Washington Square Press for permission to quote from the paperback editions of *The Family Arsenal, The Consul's File, World's End,* and *The London Embassy;* Ballantine Books for permission to quote from the paperback editions of *Girls at Play, The Great Railway Bazaar,* and *Picture Palace;* Coronet Books for permission to quote from the English paperback edition of *The Black House;* Avon for permission to quote from the paperback edition of *The Mosquito Coast;* Penguin Books for permission to quote from the English paperback edition of *Saint Jack;* G. P. Putnam's Sons for permission to quote from *O-Zone,* © 1986; and Andre Deutsch for permission to quote from *V. S. Naipaul: An Introduction to His Work.*

I am extremely grateful to Paul Theroux, who has responded swiftly and fully to my letters and requests and supplied me with information helpful to this book. He has made the entire process easier. And so have the editors at Twayne who have been thorough and extremely helpful, in particular Warren French, Athenaide Dallett, and Lewis DeSimone.

I would also like to thank Bev Chaney, Jr., inveterate book collector and new-found friend, who supplied me with information on the existent editions of Theroux's works and also with addresses, suggestions, and details that have proved to be extremely helpful. And a tip of the hat to William H. Emory, my brother-in-law, who happened to take Paul Theroux's creative writing course at the University of Virginia in the fall of 1972 and presented to me for Christmas an autographed copy of *Jungle Lovers,* my introduction to Theroux's fiction.

None of this would have been possible without the constant support and rallying cry of Emma Gray, the enthusiastic interruptions of Sam, and the abiding presence of Mavro beneath my desk. To them—and especially to Gray—must go the bulk of my indebtedness.

Chronology

1941 Paul Theroux born in Medford, Massachusetts, 10 April.

1959 Graduates from Medford High School; enters the University of Maine.

1960 Transfers to the University of Massachusetts.

1963 Graduated from the University of Massachusetts; trains for the Peace Corps at Syracuse University; sent to the Nyasaland Protectorate, which became independent Malawi in 1964.

1965 Deported from Malawi and expelled from the Peace Corps.

1966 Teaches English at Makerere University, Kampala, Uganda.

1966 Meets the writer, V. S. Naipaul, in Uganda.

1967 *Waldo,* his first novel; marries Anne Castle at the Kampala Registry Office.

1968 Leaves Africa to teach Jacobean Drama at the University of Singapore; *Fong and the Indians.*

1969 *Murder at Mount Holly; Girls at Play.*

1971 Moves to South Bowood in Dorset, England; *Jungle Lovers.*

1972 *Sinning with Annie and Other Stories; V. S. Naipaul: An Introduction to His Work;* teaches creative writing at the University of Virginia in the fall.

1973 *Saint Jack.*

1974 *The Black House.*

1975 *The Great Railway Bazaar: By Train through Asia* becomes a best-seller and the main selection of the Book-of-the-Month Club.

1976   *The Family Arsenal* chosen as a featured alternate by the Book-of-the-Month Club.

1977   *The Consul's File;* receives the award in literature from the American Academy and Institute of Arts and Letters.

1978   *Picture Palace* chosen as a featured alternate by the Book-of-the-Month Club; wins the Whitbread Award; *A Christmas Card.*

1979   *The Old Patagonian Express: By Train through the Americas* chosen as a featured alternate by the Book-of-the-Month Club; *London Snow: A Christmas Story;* writes script for the film version of *Saint Jack,* directed by Peter Bogdanovitch, starring Ben Gazzara.

1980   *World's End and Other Stories.*

1982   *The Mosquito Coast;* wins the James Tait Black Award and the Yorkshire Post Best Novel of the Year Award.

1983   *The London Embassy; The Kingdom by the Sea: A Journey around Great Britain; Sailing through China.*

1984   *Half Moon Street;* inducted into the American Academy and Institute of Arts and Letters.

1985   *Sunrise with Seamonsters: Travels and Discoveries; The Imperial Way: By Rail from Peshawar to Chittagong; Patagonia Revisited.*

1986   *O-Zone; The Mosquito Coast* filmed by director Peter Weir, starring Harrison Ford; *Half Moon Street* filmed by director Bob Swaim, starring Sigourney Weaver and Michael Caine.

Chapter One

From Medford to the World: "Travel Is Everything"

In his introduction to his collection of essays and reminiscences, *Sunrise with Seamonsters,* published in 1985, Paul Theroux wrote, "Travel is everything, and my way of travelling is completely personal. This is not a category—it is more like a whole way of life."[1] He continued: "Travel is a creative act . . . feeding the imagination, accounting for each fresh wonder."[2] It is also "a kind of discovery, and it has nothing to do with fun. It has very little to do with immediate pleasure."[3] In fact, travel has both inspired and driven Paul Theroux as a writer from the very beginning.

"I think from a very early age I had a desire to go away," Theroux wrote in discussing his own wanderlust. "I read very intensely. I had very intense imaginary experiences, and wanted both metaphorically and actually to be transported. So the desire to read and for me to lose myself in a book was the same desire that I had in traveling and losing myself in a country. Why it's there I don't know, but I think it comes from both a very strong sense of security, coming from a large, happy family, and also a desire to be an individual, to stake some sort of claim and to assert my own individuality."[4] Travel and writing became almost interchangeable pursuits, one feeding and nourishing the other: "The nearest thing to writing a novel is traveling in a strange country" (*SS,* 140). And in each the individual self emerges, conjuring up a vision of the world, themes, and plots for novels, short stories, and travel books.

In his second best-selling travel book, *The Old Patagonian Express: By Train through the Americas* (1979), Theroux described this sense of self which emerges both when he is traveling and when he is writing: "What is required is the lucidity of loneliness to capture that vision. . . . There is something in feeling abject that quickens my mind and makes it intensely receptive to fugitive impressions. . . . I craved a little risk, some danger, an untoward event, a vivid discomfort, an experience of my own company, and in a modest way the romance of solitude."[5] In travel one can discover "a fictional possibility, a situation containing both a riddle and some clues for solving it."[6] It becomes "a continuous vision, a grand tour's succession of memorable images across a curved earth" (*RB*, 82), the self in confrontation with an alien landscape, the writer in touch with created characters caught in similar situations.

And the American traveler in the second half of the twentieth century is no uprooted wanderer, no homeless creature traveling "because they belong nowhere."[7] American travelers "are made confident by the wealth of their home [in Theroux's case his sense of place rooted in a large family with six brothers and sisters], they are emboldened by their history, their literature; they are calm, they travel to compare. Travel is part of their education, and an adventure" (*N*, 77). It is moving out from a known territory, a "little risk, some danger," into a world where expatriation for the American is unknown. And it is a territory of continuing "possibilities . . . how much optimism there is here [in the United States], even in adversity, as opposed to the sense of demoralization in Western Europe."[8]

But travel suggests also escape. One can find "relief on the road, dread at his own home" (*N*, 61). Home for Paul Theroux was Medford, Massachusetts, "a drab working-class neighborhood,"[9] at 11 Belle Avenue, "infinitely like hell than earth,"[10] quipped sardonic older brother Alexander. In *Half Moon Street* (1984) Theroux described "a place that was both a town and a neighborhood of Boston . . . a barely respectable ruin of three-decker houses—dry, rust-colored shingles and sagging porches,"[11] which may suggest the Medford of his youth. Medford had once seen great days of shipbuilding; it was "a very important place in the eighteenth and nineteenth centuries, part of the triangular trade. Every person from Medford knows that; that rum and clipper ships were associated with Medford. But that's part of the oral tradition. Everyone gets that."[12] What Medford suggests to Theroux is that "uncongenial place that provides material for one's art," though he uses his hometown in a broad context (since none of his novels have actually been set there) as the kind of place to escape from. "Imagine a Medford boy like me with a crummy education, rubbing shoulders with all those fine people," Theroux wrote in 1977 to his younger brother Peter: "It goes to show you that if you keep your nose to the grindstone you won't get anywhere, because as everyone knows I got a D in algebra and used to copy my English essays out of 'The Reader's Digest.' "[13]

Youth

Theroux, born on 10 April 1941, grew up for the most part in the 1950s, which he called "one of the coldest, bleakest, stupidest decades in which to live."[14] It made the flesh of Calvin Mullet, the insurance agent in the African country of Malawi in Theroux's fifth novel, *Jungle Lovers* (1971), creep "to recall that sorry decade. . . . Those queer gray years [and] all the cool hepcats in Hudson, Mass., barfing on a six-pack of Carlings. . . . "[15] Theroux exposed his own feelings for the period and his early years in writing about a high school reunion: "In twelve years of school, I never joined a single team, wore an athlete's uniform, or competed in a sport. . . . I saw myself as bespectacled and bookish, a bit of a shut-in. . . . in fact I chose guns, bombs and fires. . . . I did not sleep with a girl until I was nineteen . . . sex was a harrowing bargain . . . it was horribly serious. . . . We had grown up in post-war dreariness and repression, expecting a cataclysm. . . . I had been a punk. . . . I knew only one thing for sure. It was this: Nothing will happen to me in Medford—worse, I will fail here. High school was proof of that. . . . I left Medford the first chance I had."[16]

The 1950s according to Theroux prescribed certain attitudes about manhood, adulthood, and growing up that he despised. For him, being a man in 1950s terms meant being "stupid. . . . unfeeling, obedient [and] soldierly."[17] Such a position "denies men the natural friendship of women. . . . It was the 1950s and if you asked too many questions about sex you were sent to camp—boy's camp, of course: the nightmare . . . prison-like . . . the quest for manliness [was] essentially right-wing, puritanical, cowardly, neurotic and fueled largely by a fear of women. It is also certainly philistine" (*SS,* 309, 310).

Being a writer in such circumstances, real or imagined, proved a hard choice for the young Theroux, undergoing that almost typically American fear of being thought different and in some way inadequate: "I found it impossible to admit to myself that I wanted to be a writer. It was my guilty secret, because being a writer was incompatible with being a man. . . . Fiction-writing is equated with a kind of dispirited failure and is only manly when it produces

wealth—money is masculinity" (*SS*, 310, 311). It was an experience
he could not easily forget: "when I was growing up, I found it very
hard to admit to myself, and impossible to admit to other people,
that I wanted to be a writer. . . . I always said, 'A doctor.' When
I went to college I was a premedical student because it was incon-
ceivable to me that I could be a writer."[18]

In his first novel, *Waldo* (1967), Waldo slowly discovers that he
wants to write, that he must write: "It's the stuff you don't know
anything about, the stuff that scares you and you're on the verge
of hating you've got to write about . . . sweaty stories, nightmares
or not."[19] Waldo spins his tale, "dazzling, uproarious, hilarious,
original, vivid" (*W*, 207). He murders his lover and opts for art:
"He could create and destroy and what he had just done in bed he
would now do on paper; he had power over life and death. . . .
You didn't have to love anyone for it though. It didn't have anything
to do with love" (*W*, 207, 208). This conviction, despite the shrill
adolescent all-or-nothing, either/or ferocity of Waldo's final decla-
ration, Theroux believes utterly.

Theroux's meeting the writer V. S. Naipaul in the English Department at Makerere University in Uganda in 1966 resulted in his
discovering both a mentor for his own writing ambitions and a
model of the consummate writer: "He was the first good writer I
had ever met. . . . It is almost impossible for me to overestimate
the importance of Naipaul's friendship then. I was 25, he was 34"
(*N*, 92). What Theroux admired about Naipaul during that first
meeting—and what he still admires—was his "fiercely independent
spirit, for his belief in himself and his talent never wavered. He
was merciless, solitary, and (one of his favorite words) unassailable"
(*N*, 94). He took note of Naipaul's powerful qualities of "doubt,
disbelief, skepticism, instinctive mistrust" (*N*, 94) and quoted Naipaul's faith in the written word: "So writing, for all its initial
distortion, clarifies, and even becomes a process of life" (*N*, 29).

And here was a wanderer, a genuine exile: "they are constantly
moving. . . . and much of their travel is flight. Rootlessness is
their condition. . . . all landscapes are alien" (*N*, 77). And a
persuasive and pervasive theme, the individual self within an alien
landscape: "The fear is of being possessed by the landscape and
imprisoned; of not being able to leave after he has successfully
escaped; the wish is to remain whole and untainted" (*N*, 74).

Lost souls in Naipaul's novels surrender to fantasies, dreams, habit, and routine, the play-acting of religion, "the mystery of meaninglessness" (*N*, 39). The writer rebels, sharpens his perceptions, masters the landscape, and moves on. Theroux pays homage to Naipaul's view of the writer as merciless solitary and quotes his mentor, who proclaimed "a freedom from people, from entanglements, from rivalries, from competition. I have no enemies, no rivals, no masters; I fear no one" (*N*, 100).

Along with Theroux's necessary "lucidity of loneliness" comes his recognition of what growing up in a large family contributed to his sense of himself as a writer: "it was not education that made me a writer, but perhaps its opposite—my sense of incompleteness, of being outside the currents of society and powerless and unprivileged and anxious to prove myself; that, and my membership in a large family, with childhood fantasies of travel . . . an isolated and hot-eyed punk" (*SS*, 3). That sense of family for Theroux provided a base, a firm foundation: "beneath this chaos there is something orderly and protective, the . . . superstructure of the extended family. . . . The pleasure of the extended family is the knowledge that one is not alone, the visible proof of love. . . . it is like a believer's satisfaction in religion."[20] "Writers often come from weak, dissembling backgrounds,"[21] Theroux once admitted, but, as we will see, his notions about the family in general permeate his fiction, if only in most places through the strong and large family's absence.

Family

Paul Edward Theroux was one of seven children of a French-Canadian father and an Italian mother. Albert Theroux, his father, now retired, worked as a salesman for the American Oak Leather Company, retailers of leather for the various shoe factories in the Northeast. His mother, Anne Dittami Theroux, paints in watercolors, loves to tell stories, and was extremely ambitious for her children. Each of Theroux's parents was one of eight children. Of both his parents Paul recalled that they really had "no place, no influence, no money nor power."[22]

Albert Theroux struggled to support his growing family. He never attended college but loved reading *Treasure Island* to his children and taking them on tours of historic sites in Boston. "My father had a lot of the actor in him," Alexander Theroux once recalled. "He may well be a descendant of some Theroux who accompanied the explorer Champlain on his second voyage to America. . . . his mother's family name, Brousseau, belonged to an illegitimate son of 'The Mad King,' Charles VI of France."[23] Paul described those French-Canadians who emigrated from Canada into Maine and New Hampshire, and who eventually ventured as far south as Providence, Rhode Island, as "hard-working but not particularly adventurous. [They chose] difficult but unimaginative occupations." [24]

For many French-Canadians the family was their entire world, separated as it often was from the world around them by language, by a strong Catholic tradition, and often by the very size of the family itself. In Rhode Island, for instance, French-Canadians attended their own parochial schools, a pattern which separated them even further from other Catholic families who attended English-speaking schools. Many worked in the textile mills, and these "difficult but unimaginative occupations" often took the place of education as an important value in terms of daily life. Such a background may have contributed to the claustrophobic atmosphere of Theroux's youth and his rebellious adolescence.

On the other hand, Anne Theroux had been graduated with honors from Lowell State College. She taught at the Hancock School, a grammar school in Medford, during the Depression and also has taught kindergarten. "My mother exhorted us to be creative," Alexander suggested. Her legacy for Paul, an outgrowth of her "generous and shrewd" nature, seems to have been his notion that "it is possible to climb."[25]

In many cases the struggling uninspired life of one's parents conjures up the more inspiring and exciting tales of grandparents. Those tales take on legendary qualities associated with the distant past and with one's own roots. Albert Theroux's father was the youngest of nine sons. When he was two in 1885 his mother was burned alive in the family farm in Quebec. By the age of thirty he at last had made it to New Hampshire, eventually got a job near Boston, and started his family.

Theroux's great-grandfather, Francesco Calesa, came from the village of Agazzano, near Piacenza in northern Italy, to New York in 1901 with his wife and four children. He hated the place and returned to Piacenza without his wife, Ermengilda, and children; "the marriage was fractured" (PE, 280–281). Ermengilda remained behind to raise the children alone "and introduced a strain of stubborn single-mindedness into the family" (PE, 281).

Asked about why so many of his sons have chosen to write, Albert Theroux once commented, "It's all because of her father." He was referring to Anne's father, Alexander Dittami. Born in Italy, Dittami was the illegitimate son of a serving-maid and an Italian senator, who went on to become ambassador to Japan and then disowned his son. The senator tried to have his son arrested, after he'd heard that Alexander had threatened to kill him; when Alexander found out, he fled to New York at the age of twenty-six. For a while he slept at the "Hotel Garibaldi," the Italians' description of the statue of Garibaldi in Central Park, before finding work and coming to Boston to open up a tailor shop and start his family. "He was a saintly, operatic man," remembers Alexander Theroux, a passionate believer in education. And Anne Theroux adds, "My father would probably have surpassed my children."[26]

"My parents seemed to believe that it was essential that none of our careers was duplicated," Paul recalls. "There would be a painter, a priest, a doctor, a nun. . . . " That essential belief has certainly been borne out. Eugene Theroux, the first-born son, born in 1939, presently lives and works in Washington, D.C., as a lawyer in the world's largest law firm, Baker and McKenzie. He acts as Paul's agent, is an expert in Sino-American trade relations, and is divorced from the writer, Phyllis Theroux. He admits that "he looks back with horror upon his father's difficult life."[27]

Alexander, the second son, born in 1940, is an established writer in his own right. Very much the aesthete, as if in reaction against his older brother's career, at present he is a writer-in-residence at the Massachusetts Institute of Technology in Cambridge. His best-known novels are *Three Wogs* (1972) and *Darconville's Cat* (1981). After high school he took the vows of silence for two years in the Trappist monastery in Spencer, Massachusetts, and went on to serve a second two years as a novice in the Franciscan seminary near Callicoon, New York. If Eugene was the establishment lawyer in the family, Alexander was to be the priest. He fled the priesthood, however, for literature.

In many ways Paul Theroux suggests a combination of his two older brothers. He has the realist's eye, the sardonic irony of a man no one can fool or appease, akin perhaps to the lawyer's sharp-eyed outlook. At the same time he has become a wealthy and critically acclaimed novelist and short-story writer. "Paul is like all new money," Alexander quipped. "He likes to talk about how much he's made."[28] Each of the three brothers has his own house on Cape Cod, near their parents.

After Paul was born in 1941, Ann-Marie, who married an Army recruiter and has two daughters, was born in 1944, and Mary, who is a registered nurse at Massachusetts General Hospital, was born in 1953. In 1955 Joseph was born. Like Paul, he joined the Peace Corps and went on to publish a first novel, *Black Coconuts, Brown Magic* in 1983. He now lives in Hawaii. Peter, born in 1957, went to Harvard and then to New College, Oxford. It is no wonder that Paul speaks often of his family, its size and influences, of "something orderly and protective," however diverse, and of that early dialectic in his own life between proving and creating his individual self and vision and celebrating and finding comfort in "the . . . superstructure of the extended family."

In *Half Moon Street* Theroux described the DeMarr family as "Catholics, and there was something about their version of Catholicism that took away their ambition and made them morally lazy: they had Heaven and the confessional and the consolations of secret rituals. There was a theatrical element in the Holy Mass, too. . . . You had to perform to be a Catholic!" (*HMS*, 150). The religion may have contributed to his notion of performance, but he rejected its dogmas and tenets early on. "Man's fate is not bound up with a belief in God," he once wrote, "but rather with a belief in man. . . . I sometimes think there is a horror of death in my fiction, and that this grows out of an absence of religion."[29]

Escape from Medford

Creature of the 1950s, a rebellious punk playing with bombs and starting fires, Theroux still was a Boy Scout as an adolescent and managed twice to be the winner of the Medford Science Fair at his high school. He was graduated in 1959, a year after Alexander, and got his wish: "I left Medford the first chance I had." As a freshman at the University of Maine the following year (1959–1960) he wrote militant anti-Vietnam War editorials that, according to Eugene, "caused his parents no end of woe."[30] Refusing to enroll in then-required Reserved Officers Training Corps, he transferred to the University of Massachusetts: "I was arrested by the campus police for leading a demonstration (that was in 1962 when demonstrations were rare and actually bothered people)."[31] In his essay on cowardice

Theroux admitted in hindsight that "It is illegal to be afraid to go into the army. . . . Fear is selfish . . . all anyone can do [is] try to be honest about what he feels, what he's seen or thinks he's seen. . . . The answers will not come by forcing ourselves upon dogma. The issue is that we should admit once and for all that we are frightened" (*SS*, 46, 47). Dogma for Theroux, any dogma, myth, cultural delusion, or public faith, became the enemy.

While at the University of Massachusetts Theroux took a creative writing course from the poet Joseph Langland. According to the writer Robert Taylor, who has interviewed Theroux several times for the *Boston Globe,* he was "enthralled by it."[32] Langland called Craig Wiley of Houghton Mifflin, and the story goes that he came to the campus and discovered Theroux sunbathing on his roof: "I gave him a novel—not a very good one, but he was impressed and said he wanted to publish my next novel, which he did four years later (This was *Waldo,* published in 1967)." Theroux went on to graduate with a Bachelor of Arts degree in 1963.

Africa

He then trained for the Peace Corps at Syracuse University. In 1963, after lecturing for a short time at the University of Urbino in Italy, he was sent to Malawi in East Africa which, at that time, was still called the Nyasaland Protectorate and administered by the British, until its independence in July 1964. He taught at Soche Hill College there and sent back sentimental articles about teaching in the bush to the *Christian Science Monitor.* He went on to write articles and poems in African, British, and American magazines, including *Esquire, Atlantic Monthly,* and *Playboy.* (He subsequently won the Playboy Editorial Award for best story four times—in 1972, 1976, 1977, and 1979.) In November 1964 an attempted coup d'etat, in which Theroux was personally involved, failed to over-throw Dr. H. Kamuzu Banda, the president-dictator of Malawi. His "plotting" involved helping the mother of David Rubadiri, a former headmaster at Theroux's school, later a delegate to the United Nations and an anti-Banda sympathizer, to flee the country. "Would I mind driving his car to Uganda," he had asked, "with his set of best china, a dinner service for twelve?"[33] During his harrowing journey Theroux was stopped at fourteen roadblocks by Banda's thugs, the Young Pioneers. He finally made it to Kampala, Uganda, talked with Rubadiri, and was persuaded to deliver an envelope to Yatuta Chisiza, the "leader of the guerrilla band, one of the most hated men in Malawi" (SS, 68).

Theroux's highly political writings in Malawi did not help matters; at one point an editorial about Vietnam, published in his own newspaper, the *Migraine,* mimeographed at the Peace Corps office, was "seized and confiscated by the American Ambassador, Sam P. Gilstrap" (SS,, 72). Nor did the discovery that, having written articles for a new German magazine, "for a year I had been working for the German equivalent of the CIA" (SS, 73). On 20 October 1965 he was deported: "Expelled is a better word, since it suggests speed" (SS, 73). He was fined for six months' unsatisfactory service by the Peace Corps, had to pay his own airfare from Blantyre back to Washington, and was then expelled from the Peace Corps.

And yet Theroux obviously discovered a liking for Central Africa: "I was a kind of nationalist. My little helps were consistent with the mood of that decade in Africa, of engaging oneself and being available for the purpose of national development" (SS, 71). He returned to teach English at Makerere University in Kampala, Uganda, lectured in the Department of Extra-Mural Studies, taught weekend courses for adults in up-country towns, and met V. S. Naipaul. As Theroux explained, "Some, like me, spent the 'sixties in the Third World—it was a way of virtuously dropping out and delicately circumventing Vietnam."[34] He lived in relative splendor, complete with a house and servants, and worked on his first novel to be published. He also met his future wife, Anne Castle, an Englishwoman from London and an Oxford graduate, who was teaching school at the time. In 1967, the same year that he met her, they were married on 4 December at the Kampala Registry Office. Their first son, Marcel, was born in Uganda in 1968. She went on eventually to produce radio programs for the BBC. Meanwhile *Waldo* had been published in the United States.

After *Waldo* had sold about four thousand copies, Theroux wrote *Fong and the Indians,* which was published in 1968 just after he left Africa. *Murder in Mount Holly* and *Girls at Play* followed, which also sold about four thousand copies, in 1969. James Atlas described *Girls at Play* as a novel about "the futility of African politics and the disintegration of tribal life."[35]

Uganda became a republic after a state of emergency was declared on 12 June 1966, and Milton Obote, the former prime minister, took over as president. Black tribes battled black tribes, a grim precursor to Idi Amin's bloody regime which was to follow. In "Scenes from a Curfew"[36] Theroux described the eeriness of experiencing life in Kampala coming to a halt, complete with the drunkenness, the distant gunshots, the easy sex, the uneasy stillness at night, and fear and loneliness. In *Sinning with Annie* (1972), his first collection of short stories, he added, "all my gestures had been scared and serious. I stopped trusting. I became rather jumpy and found I could not teach anymore. And so I left Africa."[37] He made up his mind to leave when during a demonstration a mob stoned and tried to overturn his car, in which his pregnant wife was riding with him.

Dedication to Writing

Dennis Enright, who praised *Fong and the Indians,* hired Theroux to teach at the University of Singapore: "Late in 1968 I got a job teaching at the University of Singapore. . . . I could not write about Singapore, so I wrote about Africa" (*SS,* 328, 329). He produced his fifth novel, *Jungle Lovers,* published in 1971. He wrestled with the labyrinthine plots of Jacobean drama in Singapore for three years, while his wife taught at the Chinese university. Their second son, Louis, was born there in 1969.

He realized that he must dedicate himself fully to writing, that teaching would only get in the way of that vocation, "and after working abroad for nine years as a teacher in the seasonless monotony of three tropical countries I . . . decided to chuck the whole business and never take a job again."[38] He had "regarded a book as an indulgence—I mean a 'vision' but the word sounds too pompous and spiritual" (*SS,* 2), but he remembered and admired Conrad's lines from his essay, "A Glance at Two Books": "a book is a deed. . . . the writing of it is an enterprise as much as the conquest of a colony" (*SS,* 85).

"I never wanted another job," Theroux told interviewer Charles Ruas. "My wife . . . wanted to get a job [and so I said] 'if you're going to get a job in London, I'll go,' "[39] and so they went. They moved in November 1971 to South Bowood near Bridport in Dorset and lived there, before moving up to London in April 1972. Anne continues to produce for the BBC. Theroux continues to think of Singapore in very personal terms: "My life had begun there. [It was] where one of my children was born, where I wrote three books and freed myself from the monotonous routine of teaching . . . " (*RB*, p. 236). Despite teaching a creative writing course for the fall semester in 1972 at the University of Virginia in Charlottesville, he stuck to his commitment.

True to his developing fashion—according to James Atlas, Theroux's "practice is to situate each novel in the country where he last resided"[40]—in the Dorset countryside Theroux finished his sixth novel, *Saint Jack* (1973), which was set in Singapore, went on to sell 7,500 copies, and became a film directed by Peter Bogdanovich, starring Ben Gazzara as Jack Fiori. Theroux began writing his seventh novel, *The Black House* (1974), at the University of Virginia and finished the novel in Dorset. It was later described by Robert Towers in a front-page review of *The Great Railway Bazaar* (1975) in the *New York Times Book Review* as "his most impressive novel yet . . . the macabre tale of a haunted house, of witchcraft in a remote village in Dorset."[41] It was upon completion of that novel that Theroux, "slightly cabin-crazy after [spending] a year writing [the] book, . . . as a reaction against having spent [that] year,"[42] and believing that "anything is possible on a train" (*RB*, p. 1), set out on the journey that would make him famous.

The Great Railway Bazaar, published in 1975 with a first printing of 7,500 copies, sold thirty-five thousand copies. It led to Robert Towers's front-page review in the *New York Times Book Review* on 24 August 1975: "I should like to think that there is a swelling cult of Theroux readers. . . . 'The Great Railway Bazaar' is the most consistently entertaining and the least boring book I have encountered in a long time." "It was my intention," Theroux wrote at the beginning of the book, "to board every train that chugged into view from Victoria Station in London to Tokyo Central; to take the branch line to Simla, the spur through the Khyber Pass, and the chord line that links Indian Railways with those in Ceylon; the Mandalay Express, the Malaysian Golden Arrow, the locals in Vietnam, and the trains with bewitching names, the Orient Express, the North Star, the Trans-Siberian. I sought trains; I found passengers" (*RB*, 1–2). He did it in 1973, spent Christmas of that year guzzling champagne with Russians while crossing the frozen desolation of northern Russia, and received the best critical reviews in his career up to that time, everything from "downright compelling reading" in *Publishers Weekly* to "a rare kind of book that you never want to end" in *Saturday Review. The Great Railway Bazaar* was chosen as a main selection of the Book-of-the-Month Club, became a best-seller, and earned Theroux "really the first money."[43]

Theroux continued writing. By the end of 1985 he had published three large novels, each of which was chosen as a featured alternate by the Book-of-the-Month Club: *The Family Arsenal* (1976), which sold thirty thousand copies; *Picture Palace* (1978), which received the prestigious Whitbread Award and sold forty thousand copies; and the celebrated and heralded *The Mosquito Coast* (1982), which sold about seventy-five thousand copies and won the James Tait Black Award and the *Yorkshire Post* Best Novel of the Year Award. He had also published three collections of short stories: *The Consul's File* (1977), which sold twenty thousand copies; *World's End* (1980), which sold twenty thousand copies; and *The London Embassy* (1983), which sold about the same—two long short stories, written at the suggestion of his two sons for Christmas—*A Christmas Card* (1978) and *London Snow: A Christmas Story* (1979)—and a book containing two short novels, *Half Moon Street* (1984).

He has continued writing highly successful travel books, which include *The Old Patagonian Express* (1979), a featured alternate of the Book-of-the-Month Club that sold forty-five thousand copies; *The Kingdom by the Sea* (1983), which sold about eighty-five thousand copies; the small volume, *Sailing through China* (1983); *The Imperial Way: By Rail from Peshawar to Chittagong* (1985), a "coffee-table" book complete with stunning photographs by Steve McCurry; and *Patagonia Revisited* (1985), based on a discussion between the writer Bruce Chatwin and Theroux of Patagonia's influence on literature and travelers' imaginations before the Royal Geographic Society. In 1985 he collected several of his articles and essays, written between 1964 and 1984, "meant to be concrete—responses to experiences, with my feet squarely on the ground; immediate and direct . . . and somewhat alien to the meandering uncertainties of the novel" (*SS,* 2), and published them as *Sunrise with Seamonsters: Travels and Discoveries.*

In 1977 Theroux received an Award in Literature from the American Academy and Institute of Arts and Letters—"what pleased me most," Theroux wrote, "was that John McPhee won it the same year and . . . he is a writer I admire"[44]—and on 16 May 1984 he was inducted into that august body at its headquarters on Audubon Terrace and West 155 Street in New York, along with Russell

Baker, E. L. Doctorow, and William Gaddis. He is also a Fellow of the Royal Society of Literature and the Royal Geographical Society in Britain. In 1980 he received honorary doctorates in literature from Trinity College in Washington and Tufts University in his home town, Medford. In 1986 *The Mosquito Coast* was filmed. Produced by Saul Zaentz (who also produced *Amadeus* and *One Flew over the Cuckoo's Next*) for sixteen million dollars, the film was directed by the noted Australian director Peter Weir, and starred Harrison Ford as Allie Fox. Ford received better reviews for his performance than the film itself did. *Half Moon Street* was also filmed, and Michael Caine and Sigourney Weaver starred under the direction of Bob Swaim. The film received generally negative reviews.

In 27 August 1985 it was announced in the *New York Times* that Theroux was moving to G. P. Putnam after almost twenty years with his first publisher, Houghton Mifflin in Boston. Sources disclosed that the "two-book deal—for a novel he is now working on that will come out late [in 1986] and for a travel book thereafter— is in the million-dollar range." Theroux responded, "I felt a need for change . . . things were becoming routine for me. These are my middle years, when you think of changes. . . . My life has been stimulated by change—that has been the whole point of travel."[45] Theroux also wrote, "I left Houghton Mifflin because I began to feel a sense of routinely writing and routinely turning books in; a bit like having a job. I have always disliked jobs and regular work. As I was working on a big novel it seemed an opportune time to go. Nearly all publishers' decisions are business— commercial—decisions; writers seem simply to do the best they can. But in leaving Houghton Mifflin I was making a business decision. H[oughton] M[ifflin] is a very good publisher and was very gracious to me when I left. Similarly Putnams has treated me well. I have been lucky in the people I met in publishing, but I also think I have worked hard and delivered the goods."[46]

"My life has been stimulated by change—that has been the whole point of travel." For Theroux, "Travel is everything." It is at once his passion and the touchstone of his art. It has been a long process from Medford to the world, and that process has in no way been completed, but the world knows Theroux now, and we can explore the world he has created in his art.

Chapter Two
Theroux's Art:
"A Quality of Light"

In discussing V. S. Naipaul's style, Paul Theroux declared, "Compression is Naipaul's forte . . . his eye, attentive for the smallest detail, can give an apparently common landscape or unremarkable physique many features" (N, 134,100). The detail commands Theroux's eye. In *The Great Railway Bazaar* he searches the landscape for the uncommon detail: "We passed another station. I searched it for a detail; it repeated fifty previous stations and this repetition kept it out of focus" (RB, 32). In *Picture Palace* he describes it as "a quality of light—that little kick in fiction that tells the truth and makes the rest plausible."[1] And in *The Consul's File* the consul makes it clear: "Truth is not a saga of alarming episodes; it is a detail, a small clear one, that gives a fiction life."[2]

Like many poets and novelists before him, Theroux's strategy is physiognomy, not that luminous detail that will reveal some cosmic truth but that precise look or incident or odd motion that may reveal a culture, a character, or an entire landscape. Details suggest the whole; they emerge as emblems of his characters in his fiction or of his landscapes in his travel books. He pursues them intensely, piles them up, orchestrates them in such a way that they will suggest a way of life or a character's developing personality.

The close observation of and intense concentration upon details often subvert and undermine general beliefs, ideologies, and cultural myths. Theroux casts an ironic eye upon the world around him, searching for that precise example or incident that will lay a culture bare or reveal what is really going on in a character's mind or heart, despite what he or she may believe to the contrary. In his act of discovery, whether in writing fiction or in traveling (and the two are so much a part of each other that one necessarily feeds and nourishes the other), he pursues his details, "I've torn the heart out of this place, there's nothing more to discover,"[3] and then moves on.

Theroux described this process in describing Naipaul's: "Creation, in Naipaul's terms, involves perception. The ability to assess oneself in one's setting is necessary if a person is to write well or make anything new; detail must be seen, judgments questioned, with these perceptions, the experience of something sighted, arrives a specific calmness which is resolution. In this calmness is the confident detachment which can result in creation: this still moment" (N, 15). From eying detail to judging it and one's previous perceptions comes a state of calmness, resolution, detachment, that necessary state in which the artist must work, ordering his thoughts and sentences; and from this he moves to that "still" moment of creation, a kind of ultimate recollection in tranquillity which transcribes to paper the details, the judgments, the perceptions, the overall vision. This accounts for what Robert Towers once called "the author's deadpan narrative manner,"[4] that detached eye that will not falter and calls the shots as it sees fit. And hence Susan Lardner's assessment: "Like Conrad's storyteller Charlie Marlow, Theroux has become a connoisseur of the conflict of ideals and illusions with things as they turn out to be. Irony is his natural style."[5] Dogmas of any kind kill. Details save.

Theroux juxtaposes an actual landscape or character with romantic and mythic notions about them. For example, in *The Consul's File* he attacks the self-pitying colonial creatures of Somerset Maugham's tales who are "cursed with romance": "He made heroes of these time-servers; he glorified them by being selective and leaving out their essential flaws. He gave people . . . destructive models to emulate, and he encouraged expatriates to pity themselves. It is the essence of the romantic lie" (CF, 204–6). These self-deluded people, whom we meet in his fictions and he meets in his travels, "end up having to face the fact that there is no fantasy and they're going to have to come to terms with this letdown . . . and make a few compromises."[6]

Again Theroux's perceptive critical analysis of Naipaul is important here. Naipaul's heroes are writers who perceive and create their own detached visions. His villains feed on passive fantasies: "The fantasist lives nowhere but in his dreams, which are images fed on repetitive talking [and] habitual lying. . . . they play . . . but they cannot make, and so they don't grow" (N, 44, 35). In place of true vision comes religious ritual, decadent romance, a kind of private theater based on superstition and ceremony which result only in spiritual paralysis, the support of the status quo, and a static anonymity. The individual self gets submerged in the desire "to recreate the past in fantasy" (*N*, 102), and as Naipaul suggests, "From play-acting to disorder: it is the pattern" (*N*, 38).

These patterns and confrontations often occur between individual selves—Theroux's fictional characters and his own traveling persona—and alien landscapes. "I often find that an alien landscape comes to me in sharper focus," Theroux wrote in 1979, "and I like contrast: of character or situation."[7] He would probably agree with W. J. Harvey's notions of realistic characters in novels as those individuals operating within their own sense of conditional freedom, a kind of equilibrium between the self and the world, between their own free will and the determinism forced upon them by circumstance, between choice and chance.[8] Frederick Karl expands this notion, referring to Theroux as master of "the encounter, the scene, the techniques of blending past and present." Theroux's is "the world of travel books, journeys, chance encounters."[9] In "A Love-Scene After Work" (1971) Theroux amplifies his position: "the place is so different I can indulge myself in long unbroken reflections, for the moments of observation are still enough to allow the mind to travel in two directions. . . . In a foreign country I can live in two zones of time . . . slowly, in a foreign place, the memory whirrs and gives back the past . . . juxtaposed with the vivid present it is an acute reminder of my estrangement."[10] The emblematic encounter: details versus myths, the self versus an alien landscape, the past versus the present, the "deadpan" ironic style versus cultural faiths and ideologies. This encounter lies at the heart of Theroux's art.

These landscapes are not just any landscapes in the world or of the soul. They are, as Susan Lardner describes them, "unsettled and godforsaken outposts," and "Theroux operates . . . as a kind of secret agent, transmitting messages from [there]."[11] Theroux makes this clear: "I am fascinated by societies in the process of change. We in America are unfamiliar with drastic change and deterioration."[12] "I liked living in places which were changing, either had been something, or were in the process of becoming something else, or were in complete decline . . . places that were becoming decolonized, or facing the prospect of war, or just had a war. . . . The people are at the edge . . . [drawn] to the idea of just wildness or emptiness, or social decrepitude—all of that is interesting."

Theroux's world reflects what has come to be called "Third World," in many cases the "Fourth World," that place, akin to Naipaul's, where "people are doomed . . . they are much worse off [after decolonization] than anyone thought conceivable." It is a postimperial world, a shattered, broken, and disheveled place where poverty and hunger stun the onlooker in the apparent omnipotent inevitability of their dangerous and frightening reign. "I don't have any nostalgia for empire, or any illusions about freedom,"[13] Theroux insists, but such a place "spawns desperate people. You can hate oppression, as V. S. Naipaul said, but fear the oppressed."[14]

It is a world for which the West remains in many ways responsible. "The Third World is a version of Hell: the West has had a hand in shaping it,"[15] Theroux once commented. "We have colonized their subconscious." His subject focuses on the implications of our own culture in the rest of the world.

The individual self in Theroux's world, who must face and tackle these implications if he or she is to survive in such a place, is not all that straightforward. There are Theroux's innocents, usually Americans, trapped in circumstances beyond their countrol, armed only with a kind of American promise that the territory they are in utterly rejects, such as Calvin Mullet, the insurance agent in *Jungle Lovers,* Bettyjean Lebow, the Peace Corps teacher, who pays with her life in *Girls at Play,* (both novels take place in Africa), and even the seemingly worldly Lauren Slaughter, the Dr. Slaughter of *Half Moon Street* in a dreary wintry London. More worldly characters, or those so obsessed with their own cranky visions of the world that they can see nothing else, battle with the elements: Jack Fiori of Singapore, Alfred Munday in Dorset, Valentine Hood in grimy southeast London, the consul Spencer Savage in Malaysia and diplomatic London, Maude Coffin Pratt imprisoned by her querulous notions of art and the shadows of her own past, and Allie Fox in the Honduran jungle, determined to reinvent the world that God left unfinished. And one should include Theroux's own self-image in his travel books that Robert Towers has described as "acerbic, bookish, deadpan, observant, bibulous and rather passive. . . . He can be cranky."[16]

The individual can suffer from his own preoccupations with his own perceptions and find himself cut off from the world around him. Characters such as Alfred Munday in *The Black House,* Miss Poole and Heather Monkhouse in *Girls at Play,* even Maude Pratt in *Picture Palace* and both Charles and Allie Fox in *The Mosquito Coast*, discover how easily they can become enclosed in their own doubts and fears, victimized by Gothic shadows and their own solipsistic uncertainties. Anarchy threatens practically everyone in *The Family Arsenal*, and many characters in Theroux's short stories find themselves stalking tombs, experiencing hallucinations, being stalked by nightmare creatures, attempting murder, and fearing strange fevers and other midnight horrors. "My real weakness is for a well-made ghost story," Theroux once admitted. "I like M. R. James very much. . . . I like Poe."[17] In describing the process of writing, he commented, "By stages one encloses oneself in one's novel, erects a barrier that shuts out the real world to duplicate it" (*SS*, 85). In that self-enclosure stranger perceptions and fears can fester and grow.

Theroux celebrates that "lucidity of loneliness" in which to conjure up his perceptions that lead to vision, but that solitary state can easily slip over into something darker, into a kind of hypnagogic state between waking and sleeping in which the traveler loses contact with the world around him and often with himself. In *The Great Railway Bazaar* Theroux describes this "trancelike state. Extensive traveling induces a feeling of encapsulation; and travel, so broadening at first, contracts. . . . [It left me with] my failing memory and a kind of squinting fear I took to be an intimation of paranoia. The jungle was thick" (*RB*, 221). Many of Theroux's characters are never very far from "the symptoms of encapsulated terror" (*RB*, 275), that "mental motion-sickness" (*RB*, 279) that often pursues them. It is a glimpse of some terrible loneliness, a solitude no amount of social intercourse can cure. They stalk strange outposts and come upon their own isolated shadows.

Throughout Theroux's fiction and his travel books a pervasive existential emptiness threatens to undermine the observer and the soul. Some black house of the self shivers just beneath the surface of other quests and the speed of trains, as if the landscape were possessing it instead of the other way round. It is as if the self had become a function of what it was seeing, no longer the cause of that vision. As early as *Waldo* we come upon "the little dry house" within the self that people name the "heart, soul, ego, which did not interest Waldo at all" (*W*, 50). A new neighborhood will direct our attentions elsewhere. After the long journey "by train through the Americas" Theroux arrives at Patagonia: "I knew I was nowhere.

. . . [I saw] enormous empty spaces. . . . You had to choose between the tiny or the vast. . . . *Nowhere is a place"* (*PE,* 403). Could his thirst for detail suggest an evasion of "enormous empty spaces" and "the little dry house" within? In *Girls at Play* Bettyjean Lebow discovers, "In the silence was all of Africa's cruel ambiguity, what people took for mystery; it was not mystery . . . but empty."[18] The consul Spencer Savage agrees: "We tend to see mystery in emptiness, but I knew from Africa that emptiness is more often just that: behind it is a greater emptiness" (*CF,* 207). And in *The Kingdom by the Sea* Theroux's praise is reserved for Cape Wrath, the northwestern tip of Scotland, "an eerie landscape. . . . It was not picturesque and it was practically unphotographable . . . at times it seemed diabolical. . . . It was stunningly empty. . . . I was happy. . . . I felt safe here."[19]

Perhaps such emptiness, however flat or majestic, reflects our own ultimate demise, a mystery into which each of us must finally sink. "I sometimes think there is a horror of death in my fiction," Theroux wrote, " and that grows out of an absence of religion. . . . As I was raised a Catholic I have a deep respect for people who have Faith; but I have none myself."[20] From such horrors, details may provide a temporary sanctuary.

"I like a plotty novel. . . . I believe in clarity . . . of language and form,"[21] Theroux wrote, and his fiction reveals this. His novels divide into well-balanced parts and are usually sectioned off accordingly. Image patterns reveal a carefully crafted equilibrium between order and chaos, black and white, England and Africa, the American consciousness and the East. Even his characters provide this essential duality: Monkhouse and Poole in *Girls at Play,* Mullet and Marais in *Jungle Lovers,* Fiori and Leigh in *Saint Jack,* Hood and Weech in *The Family Arsenal,* Charles and Allie Fox in *The Mosquito Coast,* and perhaps at its most deliberate Maude and Orlando Pratt in *Picture Palace*—and in the text of that entire novel, as explored in detail by Robert F. Bell[22]—and the twins DeMarr in "Dr. DeMarr" from *Half Moon Street.*

Doubling reigns supreme, at times almost in the allegorical manner of American romance, as practiced by Hawthorne and Melville, Joan Didion and Norman Mailer, in which characters become polarized opposites and exist as shadows and/or mirrors of one another. Thus the passive Mullet encounters the revolutionary Marais; Maude Pratt's photographic art both reveals and conceals her own life and literally produces doubles of the people she meets. Heather Monk-house represents everything Miss Poole does not and threatens her very existence by her mere presence at the school in the African bush. Alfred Munday is haunted by a succubus-like lover in *The Black House* and watches Dorset and Africa, seeming opposites, becoming more and more alike, as he sinks into his own darker fantasies. Fathers haunt sons; anarchists threaten whatever urban order remains; blacks and whites find themselves entangled in racist dialectics that produce both hatred and need.

And each main character struggles with his or her alien environment, whether it be Africa, Singapore, England, a decaying London, or even one's own memories. "The general idea of the secret sharer occurs again and again in the novels and stories,"[23] Susan Lardner suggests. Duplicity appears everywhere. And Theroux's "plotty" novels in their carefully balanced structures reproduce and reflect these haunting duplicities.

Robert L. Caserio argues that plot by its very nature implies transformation and purpose, narrative acts that carry with them moral values. Plotless novels, those most associated with modernist writers such as James Joyce, reveal a distrust of self, of purposeful action, and therefore strike Caserio as bypassing life's essential structure of meaning, that sense of struggling to make life coherent and significant.[24] Whether this follows or not is not essential here, but it does echo Theroux's suggestion as to why Valentine Hood and Jack Fiori act the way they ultimately do in *The Family Arsenal* and *Saint Jack:* "I would suggest that Hood and Jack Flowers don't see an alternative to acting ethically: they are compelled by the rightness of the act. . . . Fiction gives us the second chance that life denies us, so this 'right thought' is I suppose something personal. I would like to act correctly—I mean, have the strength to make moral decisions without hesitation."[25]

Caserio also makes another point that may illuminate Theroux's fictional structures. He suggests that the novelist's connection with his plot may be similar to a parent's or child's to his family. And consequently those novelists who create "anti-plots" may be doing so to subvert "the *authority* of contemplative designs of life,"[26] as the child might attack and overthrow the parent. If we can extend this idea in relation to Theroux's fiction, we might think that Theroux's tight and well-balanced plots may reveal his celebration and reliance upon his own extended family. Despair and emptiness are "remedied" by the well-balanced plot, by the "poetic justices" of the text itself. Everything comes out well-rounded and cleverly crafted: there are no loose ends. Darker themes and visions are held in this net, as the individual self may be supported by the "super-structure of the extended family. . . . beneath this chaos there is something orderly and protective."[27]

The family arsenal may disclose doubts and uncertainties—"The secret theme . . . [may be] that parents . . . are in fact the wrathful tigers who inadvertently consume their children"[28]—but the family plot ultimately holds them all in its wide embrace. As Theroux wrote about his own large family, despite his self-doubts "of being outside the currents of society and powerless and unprivileged and anxious to prove myself," in the last analysis "one is not alone. . . . it is like a believer's satisfaction in religion" (*SS,* 167). That is the most open confession of faith Theroux has made, other than in his own art as a dedicated writer, and it may reveal some of the reasons for the "plottiness" of that art.

"I'm obsessed with knowing what I'm writing about," Theroux asserts. "I think I am a very deliberate writer and rewriter; and I know that my writing is not accidental. . . . I try . . . to practice precision."[29] This note of deliberation and precision Theroux sounds over and over again. It matches in intensity his focus upon the telling detail, the revealing incident. "Slowly, it happens," he continues, "a phrase, a sentence, a paragraph. Nothing comes out right the first time, and you are not so much writing as learning a language . . . recopying, rewriting, beginning again, and understanding that it will take a long time" (*SS,* 86). He adds: "I write in longhand so I can memorize everything I've written; committing a novel to memory makes it possible to think about it, extend it, and correct it in any idle hour" (*SS,* 85).

The emphasis on control and solitude permeates Theroux's notions of writing: "Writing is pretty crummy on the nerves. There's no glamour in it. . . . If you still feel like writing, you realize that it's going to keep you out of society." And it is necessary to en-capsulate oneself in this process, as referred to above: "By stages one encloses oneself in one's novel, erects a barrier that shuts out the real world to duplicate it" (*SS,* 85). Travel comes to the rescue of the solitary writer—he admits to being "slightly cabin-crazy after writing"—but even on his train rides around the world, he works on further encounters, other books: "If you're writing, you have to

offer yourself and create an occasion, and it's a very exhausting thing
. . . ."[30] "Travel . . . has very little to do with immediate pleasure."[31] The writer remains ever on the alert, as if determined to
possess and conjure up a landscape or a character before they possess
him, forever "allied to a fiercely independent spirit," Theroux wrote
about Naipaul, "for his belief in himself and his talent never wavered" (*N*, 94).

"All anyone can do [is] try to be honest about what he feels,"
Theroux wrote in "Cowardice" (1967), "what he's seen or thinks
he's seen. . . . The answers will not come by forcing ourselves
upon dogma."[32] And he must be honest about all things: "The issue
is that we should admit once and for all that we are frightened"
(*C*, 47). That honesty underscores Theroux's fascination with detail,
perception, that calm detachment, without which creation is impossible; the confrontation between an individual and an alien landscape, the American innocent doomed by his or her inadequacies
and insufficiencies; the fear of solipsism and disconnection; the threat
of emptiness and the haunted sense of being possessed rather than
possessing; and the carefully orchestrated scaffolding of plot and
structure, the extended fortifications of the whole.

Questions necessarily arise, which we will examine in closer detail
in relation to specific books. On the one hand, in his criticism of
Naipaul's vision, Theroux explains that the fantasist, submitting
himself to religious rites and rituals, surrendering to superstitions
and ceremonies, in effect supports the status quo. He changes nothing; he is a mere prisoner of "romance, awe and mystery. It is the
mystery of meaninglessness" (*N*, 39). The man of vision, on the
other hand, moves from details seen to judgments rendered, from
perceptions registered to creation achieved. But if surrendering to
fantasy leads to paralysis and a static anonymity, and fresh perception
leads to vision and understanding, how is one to tell the difference?
And doesn't the latter resist change as much as the former? Don't
they, in effect, both uphold the status quo by lodging fantasy and/
or true vision securely within the mind and, therefore, "disconnected" from the status quo without? Couldn't the vision of decay,
disorder, and futility itself be a fantasy, a dark rendering of a self
not plunging forward into understanding but retreating into a complacent melancholy or despair? And couldn't the ferocity of "detail-
mongering" be seen as a momentary stay against confusion, not as
a journey toward some revelation? If one reproduces a vision of

decay, isn't that in some way evading the issue and joining those
darker forces the fantasist supposedly worships blindly?

Can Theroux's plots sometimes blunt his vision? And his splen-
didly readable lines evade moral issues instead of reveal them? Frederick Karl suggests that Theroux "turns casual when intensity and
gravity are needed. He chooses 'writing'—clean prose, good approaches, readability—over the true angulation his material calls
for. . . . The result is a novel at the level of adventure, whose
interest derives from exotic settings, sensual surfaces (no love, no
pain, inflicted or received), and wisecracks which often suffice for
conversation. This is the world of travel books, journeys, chance
encounters."[33] While readability is hardly a crime, the issue is a
real one and requires further exploration.

Robert Towers feels that Theroux's tone, his "deadpan narrative
manner can usually be counted on to keep his indignation under
control,"[34] but often irony spills over into sardonic and shrill name-
calling. Irony presents an often thin wire on which to perch; one
lapse in the tone, and the detachment, the balancing act, is lost.
Recent critics have complained of Theroux's persona in his travel
books, such as in *The Kingdom by the Sea*. Frequently we hear his
voice and manner called "misanthropic"[35] "jaundiced,"[36] "dyspep-
tic,"[37] and "sneering."[38] At one point Anatole Broyard couples
Theroux with Naipaul as writers who "go abroad to refine [their]
disgust."[39]

In his novels Theroux seems to work best when he is able to
create a strong central character, writhing with indignation and
querulous vituperation, and to distance himself from that character.
He himself once explained, "My heroes are people who have carried
out difficult journeys single-handedly. . . . It is not the macho
element, but the courage, the confidence [and] the planning."[40] One
thinks of Maude Pratt's testy grumblings; Allie Fox's mad assaults
on his native land, on scavengers and God; Valentine Hood's smoldering rage; Alfred Munday's cranky complaints; and Lauren Slaughter's half-witted condescension and put-downs. Perhaps Theroux
occupies some place close by, torn between railing against the in-
justices and tawdriness of the contemporary scene, like some furious
Old Testament prophet, and exorcising some curiously consummate
wrath within himself. Pratt must face her incestuous past; Fox has
his tongue torn out by vultures; Munday loses his wife and his
demonic succubus-mistress; Lauren Slaughter barely escapes with

her life. As Caserio suggests, despite Theroux's public praise of the extended family, "Parenthood and family structure are explosively irrational. They are the mask of an essential anarchy of intense feelings. . . . The perfect weapon has been long invented and established: it is family man and family plot."[41] Perhaps these irrational feelings may surface in these querulous characters. Only Hood, "St. Jack," Mullet, Waldo, and Fong manage to "escape" and in their own way "triumph" over circumstances and, in some instances, themselves.

And yet, as Susan Lardner describes it, "Traveling [and I would add, writing], Theroux has tested a belief in the continuing strangeness of the world, and discovered openings for melodrama and romantic gestures that other writers have given up for lost. Characters entangled in the coils of a plot, feeling their way through a pointed sequence of events, reflect his experience of the unexpected and of unpredictable destinations."[42] And these characters, in W. J. Harvey's terms, really are in most cases "something more than a creation of language or a function in the total context of the play. [They] elude[] and def[y] classification [because of their] ultimately enigmatic nature . . . what we mean by the character's *life*."[43]

"Man's fate is not bound up with a belief in God, but rather with a belief in man,"[44] Theroux asserted and whether true or not proves it again and again in the context of his fiction. That sense of discovering the strange and the unexpected, that older sense of the novel taking the reader to new or further places, Theroux has mastered in his lean, clipped prose style. We can chart the growth of that discovery from its first rumblings in *Waldo* to its triumph in *The Mosquito Coast*. "The movement of travel is merciful," Theroux wrote in *The Old Patagonian Express* (*PE,* 9), and we should look first at the travel books to explore that kind of discovery that is the focal point of Theroux's art.

Chapter Three
The Travel Books: "Movement . . . Is Merciful"

What Theroux describes as "the lazy indulgence of travel for its own sake" in *The Great Railway Bazaar* (*RB*, 32), becomes in *The Old Patagonian Express*, "the movement of travel is merciful" (*PE*, 9). The journey itself is all: "What interests me is the waking in the morning, the progress from the familiar to the slightly odd, to the rather strange, to the totally foreign, and finally to the outlandish. The journey, not the arrival, matters" (*PE*, 5). Theroux's interest coincides with "the going and the getting there, in the poetry of departures" (*PE*, 383), and in the open-endedness and perpetual renewal and possibility that travel suggests: "We were far from home: we could be anyone we wished. Travel offers a great occasion to be the amateur actor" (*PE*, 74).

In *The Kingdom by the Sea* (1983) travel suggests ultimate flight, running away from home, escape—"I liked thinking that I was always making *progress* whenever I walked away"[1]—and finally the notion that "[a]ll travelers are optimists, I think. Travel itself was a sort of optimism in action" (*KS*, 130). "To be anonymous and traveling in an interesting place is an intoxication" (*KS*, 120). Thus the travel book becomes the tale of "the loner bouncing back bigger than life to tell the story of his experiment with space. It is the simplest sort of narrative, an explanation which is its own excuse for the gathering up and the going. It is *motion* given order by its repetition in words" (italics mine, *PE*, 3).

Though Robert Towers described Theroux as a writer who "staked out for himself a fictional terrain that is generally thought of as British," the postimperial "third" world, and though Theroux's first travel book struck Towers as belonging "to an English tradition, that of the eccentric travel book,"[2] Theroux's spiritual allegiances suggest his own American heritage. The motion of travel for its own sake, the notions of progress and optimistic discovery, the sensation of flight and escape, the loner experimenting with space: such descriptions of travel reveal Theroux's Americanness.

The American myth shimmers with notions of self-renewal, rebirth, self-made men, the visible grace of going and doing, that sense of ultimate hope in which most things are supposed to progress and expand, including the lone self which confronts a wilderness or an alien landscape and conquers it in terms of his own perceptions or his masterful technological skills. American literature and history are filled with "the succession of exoduses, at once repetitive and developmental, that would culminate in the exodus from history itself,"[3] suggests Sacvan Bercovitch: the self can master all things and transcend the circumstances of the everyday, of history. Though the individual may look out upon a world in decay and despair, he can move on and in doing so "rise above" or at least beyond circumstantial "traps."

Theroux, however, harbors no dogmatically transcendent faith. However romantic his notion of the individual self may be, it is still anchored to the precision of his perceptions and his language. In this he seems almost Puritan, "insisting upon the exclusive primacy of words" as deeds, as Larzer Ziff explains. Ziff goes on to explore the Puritans' fascination with the written word: "The written word, which had begun the revolution in consciousness that gave birth to their culture, was still the central way of apprehending reality . . . words themselves exerted a near-magical power. To control them was to control the essence of what they designated."[4]

The American romantic faith lives in Theroux's sense of travel and the self. The American Puritan tradition lives in his precise faith in language, in the ability of words to conjure up a place, a people, a continent, and attach significant meaning to them, to make them ultimately signify.

Travel for Theroux is a mode of perception and a precise task, a romantic expression and a puritanical proof of meaning. He defined this kind of travel in *The Kingdom by the Sea*: "[I]t was travel, perhaps in a new sense but in an old place, because I was looking hard at it for the first time and making notes, and because I had no other business there" (*KS,* 36). "Travel was, above all, a *test* of memory," he wrote in *The Old Patagonian Express* (italics mine, *PE,* 337); "I knew I was merely skimming south, a bird of passage generalizing on the immediate. But because I had no camera and had written so much, my impressions of what I had seen were vivid" (*PE*, 337). The skimming, the passing, provides the romantic faith in the progress of motion and renewal; the "looking hard," the "test," and the writing "so much" prove the significance of self-perception, the true calling of his vocation.

On the last page of *The Great Railway Bazaar* Theroux emphasizes the work of travel: "I had worked every day, bent over my rocking notebook like Trollope scribbling between postal assignments . . ." (*RB*, 342). On travel writing itself he explained, "If you're writing, you have to offer yourself and create an occasion, and it's a very exhausting thing."[5] Upon these occasions Theroux builds his travel books: "I . . . think that I try to bring novelistic techniques into building a scene—and dialogue. From the beginning, I've always tried to write travel with a tremendous amount of dialogue so that one hears people, hears the voice, hears the characteristic way the people speak."[6] The work of travel involves recording these emblematic encounters, the voices of other people, the telling detail that reveals a landscape, a country, and a culture. As he described it in *The Great Railway Bazaar*: "I sought trains; I found passengers" (*RB*, 2).

As Bercovitch writes about the American Puritan, "He earns his authority as communal spokesman not by his relation to any existent community, but by personal assertion. His myth is essentially projective and elite . . . [and his duty is] to impose prophecy upon experience."[7] That notion of Puritan authority and American work illuminates Theroux's own.

Theroux's active pursuit of the strange world around him and the self within animates his imagination: "I traveled easily in two directions, along the level rails while Asia flashed changes at the window, and at the interior rim of a private world of memory and language. I cannot imagine a luckier combination" (*RB*, 166). Ultimately travel is both "a continuous vision, a grand tour's succession of memorable images across a curved earth [and] is circular. . . . The farther one traveled, the nakeder one got, until, towards the end, ceasing to be animated by any one scene, one was most oneself" (*RB*, 82, 341, 297). Landscape and the self interpenetrate one another to the point of vision: "it is every traveler's conceit that no one will see what he has seen: his trip displaces the landscape, and his version of events is all that matters. He is certainly kidding himself in this, but if he didn't kid himself a little, he would never go anywhere" (*PE,* 352).

That self is specifically animated by train travel: "Anything is possible on a train. . . . Those whistles sing bewitchment: railways are irresistible bazaars, snaking along perfectly level no matter what the landscape, improving your mood with speed. . . . The train can reassure you in awful places" (*RB,* 1). On the train Theroux can seek that solitude, that sense of detachment and calm, that he so often links to the creative process. While all airplane rides strike Theroux as grimly similar, "the trains in any country contain the essential paraphernalia of the culture. . . . [They represent] the society so completely that to board [them] was to be challenged by the national character" (*RB,* 209). And even though the terrible trains of South America are jammed with Indians and the poor—"there was a class stigma attached to the trains" (*PE,* 283)—still for Theroux, "It helps to take the train if one wishes to understand. . . . The train had given me a sense of continuity . . . unlike the dislocation and disconnection one experiences after a plane journey" (*PE,* 103, 102).

Theroux is no railway buff, as he makes perfectly clear in *The Kingdom by the Sea.* Trains as trains, disconnected from the journey and his contemplation, offer nothing special to him. "The trouble with railway buffs was that they were not really interested in going anywhere. . . . They liked the atmosphere" (*KS,* 137, 138), but as he says about Stan Wigbeth, "like many other railway buffs, he detested our century" (*KS,* 175). "It was the railway buffs who were helping to dismantle British Railways. Their nostalgia was dangerous, since they hankered for the past and were never happier than when they were able to turn an old train into a toy" (*KS,* 335). It is the train in league with the actual journey, the object in motion, that Theroux celebrates, much as he celebrates the ongoing progress of travel itself.

What exactly is that "self" Theroux conjures up in his travel books, that persona who observes and passes judgment so readily? To Robert Towers, Theroux adopts an "acerbic, bookish, deadpan, observant, bibulous and rather passive" persona in *The Great Railway Bazaar.* "He can be cranky with fellow passengers . . . [he] has the courage of his national prejudices . . . [and his] deadpan narrative manner can usually be counted on to keep his indignation under control."[8] He remains always sharp-eyed and at times sharp-tongued, searching for that ironic angle of vision that will upend certain prejudices, cultural myths, and usual expectations. He is hard on willfully ignorant tourists, would-be con artists, and complacent people of any stripe. As he makes clear in *The Kingdom by the Sea,* "I cultivated complainers" (*KS,* 71). His is the eye stripped of romantic lenses, for most of his landscapes "had so seldom been seen plainly" (*KS,* 343).

Theroux works diligently to discover sharp revealing images or snatches of dialogue that bristle with a clear-eyed irreverence, thus avoiding that kind of sentimental reverence found all too easily in most popular travel writing. Here are some lines selected from a national magazine about other cultures and countries: "As in the villages, before people drink tea someone flicks a few drops into the air, an offering to the spirits. Cold evenings in the high-pasture country are magical as shepherd families gather around a fire beneath the stars. Men with braided hair ask me why night follows day and I illustrate my reply by walking around the low blaze turning a potato in the firelight."[9] Implicit in these few sentences is a sentimentalized pastoral vision of a simpler life, a nobler people, something "magical" in the family gathering around the fire. The observer here seems to long for that gathering, implicitly wishing to become a part of it. He moves in with his potato to join the group. A simplistic sense of awe and wonder permeates the elegaic rhythms of the long lines of the passage and stirs up a sigh of regret in the excluded visitor's o'erburdened memory.

In contrast here is Theroux describing the Indians in church in Ecuador, a scene that all too easily could fall prey to the sentiments above: "These churches were filled with Indians on their knees, praying in ponchos and shawls, carrying papooses . . . they were venerating the guitar of Ecuador's first saint. . . . No one could explain the guitar; a guitar requires no explanation in South America. The Indians gazed on it; they were small, stout, bandy-legged, with thick black hair, like kindly trolls. They walked bent over even when they were carrying nothing: it is a carrier's posture" (*PE,* 274–75). In Theroux's description we see real hair, "thick" and "black" as opposed to the gentler and more generalized "braided" in the previous passage. Theroux remains an observant outsider at all times and pokes fun not at the people but at the objects of their veneration, in this instance the guitar of Santa Mariana de Jesus. He has a keen sense of social injustice, of the Indians' real place in the Ecuadorian social hierarchy. He does not view them in some romantic halo of "magical" light, divorced from social realities and raised to positions of sentimentalized icons.

Implicit in Theroux's approach to his subjects is an elevated sense of distance, that necessary distance cultivated by irony and frequently disdain. He admires Naipaul's ability to submerge himself in his subject: "He composes in the shadows of the landscape, never outlining his own figure. In an encounter, it is the person encountered who is sketched, not himself. . . . The technique is a skillful suppression of his own personality; it allows his surroundings to loom" (*N,* 81). But Theroux always—and perhaps more honestly—draws attention to himself, his illnesses, his gin, his discomfort, his often querulous self-regard under difficult or trying circumstances. The wider-eyed "innocence" and delight often found in *The Great Railway Bazaar* all too often degenerates into the grouchy comments and surly grumblings in *The Kingdom by the Sea.* Railways may be "irresistible bazaars," but they can also lead to dull towns, empty hotels, the sardonic quip to shut someone up, and the derisively sweeping generality that often smacks of stereotypical name-calling and backbiting.

Theroux's sense of self includes a darker, more fascinating side often not found in travel books. It is obviously his vehicle of vision:

It is hard to see clearly or to think straight in the company of other people. Not only do I feel self-conscious, but the perceptions that are necessary to writing are difficult to manage when someone close by is thinking out loud. . . . What is required is the *lucidity of loneliness* to capture that vision. . . . There is something in feeling abject that quickens my mind and makes it intensely receptive to fugitive impressions. . . . Travel is not a vacation. . . . I craved a little risk, some danger, an untoward event, a vivid discomfort, an experience of my own company, and in a modest way the romance of solitude. (italics mine, *PE,* 169)

Theroux's "lucidity of loneliness," that modest "romance of solitude," lies at the heart of his enterprise. Only the self alone can see; other selves blur and distort, as do other versions of previous visions, other reports, and other prophecies and myths. Vision depends on an ultimate self-reliance, the loner's quest to see plainly:

So only I was left, like Ishmael: "And I only am escaped alone to tell thee". . . . If one of the objects of travel was to give yourself the explorer's thrill that you were alone . . . . a solitary mission of discovery in a remote place, then I had accomplished the traveler's dream. . . . You look around; you're alone. It is like arriving. In itself it is like discovery. . . . In the best travel books the word *alone* is implied on every exciting page. . . . Alone, alone: it was like proof of my success. I had had to travel very far to arrive at this solitary condition. (*PE*, 391)

And yet the corollary to this romance of solitude becomes a kind of self-encapsulation, an isolation so strong and overwhelming it suggests Hawthorne's haunted mind, the imagination become a passive mirror unable to rid itself of its own fears of death and self-destruction. Glimpses of this state surface in *The Great Railway Bazaar*. Theroux describes "the symptoms of encapsulated terror" (*RB*, 275), a Poesque sensation of entrapment and trance: "Extensive traveling induces a feeling of encapsulation; and travel, so broadening at first, contracts the mind"; he experienced a "kind of squinting fear I took to be an intimation of paranoia" (*RB*, 221), a kind of "mental motion-sickness" (*RB*, 279) and claustrophobia that leads to stranger dreams: "The dream was an intimation of panic, guilty traveling, and a loneliness that made me lonelier still when I wrote it and examined it" (*RB*, 323).

In *The Old Patagonian Express* Theroux reveals this state more completely, as if he had become more self-consciously aware of the darker price of travel, that sense of motion that is not merciful or intoxicating, thereby not sparing even himself from his careful scrutinies: "Travel is a vanishing act, a solitary trip down a pinched line of geography to oblivion" (*PE*, 3), and the self can rescue itself only by writing a travel book, delighting in "the loner bouncing back bigger than life to tell the story of his experiment with space." Yet he often feels in his travels like "an intruder, a stranger watching people go through familiar motions that I could not affect or enter into. . . . I had a sense of having deserted my responsibilities" (*PE*, 191); and as a profiteer, a voyeur: "We were all profiteering in the New World, even I with my leak-proof shoes and my notebooks was plundering the place with my eyes and hoping to export a few impressions" (*PE*, 282).

Theroux is drawn mysteriously to the edge of things, as if lured to discover some wasteland or emptiness within himself: "Perhaps this explained my need to seek out the inscrutable magnetisms of the exotic: in the wildest place everyone looked so marginal, so temporary, so uncomfortable, so hungry and tired, it was possible as a traveler to be anonymous or even, paradoxically, to fit in, in the same temporary way" (*PE,* 192). It is an urge toward some ultimate place and knowledge, toward some stripped-down essential self to see what makes it tick. It is a quest to examine perception itself, to see how far it will take him, where it will lead, and what it can ultimately bring back.

Theroux quotes John Donne, "Solitude is a torment which is not threatened in hell itself" (*PE,* 295). Trapped high in the mountains of Colombia, where "there was no road, no valley, no mountains, no sky, only a gray sea kingdom of mist," he experienced "a species of blindness, of blind flight . . . enchantment so pure and unexplainable that I lost all sense of space and time. It was most of all like an experience of death. . . . I could see nothing but a grave featureless vapor, my senses in collapse" (*PE,* 257). And the scene struck him "like the horror scene that greets Arthur Pym at the end of his voyage," that annihilating "white-out" at the end of Poe's longest tale (*PE,* 257).

Theroux scrutinizes his essential fears, as he scrutinizes the people and landscapes he passes by and through: "There are many satisfactions in solitary travel, but there are just as many fears. The worst is the most constant: it is the fear of death . . . every day I knew this fear. . . . I had left a safe place and had journeyed to a dangerous one. The risk was death. . . . I was a solitary explorer in a strange land" (*PE,* 394, 395). "I would not deny that there are fears indicated in my work," he once wrote, "perhaps many more than I can see. . . . There is a horror of death in my fiction."[10]

The Great Railway Bazaar: By Train through Asia (1975): "The Railway Was a Fictor's Bazaar"

In his first travel book Theroux embarks on his first journey with relish and delight. There's a kind of bemused innocence in his approach, an unjaded enthusiasm for the journey itself: "It was my intention to board every train that chugged into view from Victoria Station in London to Tokyo Central; to take the branch line to Simla, the spur through the Khyber Pass, and the chord line that links Indian Railways with those in Ceylon; the Mandalay Express, the Malaysian Golden Arrow, the locals in Vietnam, and the trains with bewitching names, the Orient Express, the North Star, the

Trans-Siberian" (*RB*, 1–2). He admits, "I was embarked on a fairly aimless enterprise" (*RB*, 32), but the enterprise is all, and the brisk, swift narrative pace speeds the reader on his way.

From such a delightful book one wants to quote in full Theroux's impressions of everything from Venice to Calcutta, from Peshawar to Siberia. Descriptions leap off the page, including his perceptions of countries, people, conditions, and landscapes. We see "the moghul and colonial splender" of Lahore (*RB*, 86) and enjoy the notion that "modernization stopped in Turkey with the death of Ataturk, at five minutes past nine on November 10, 1938" (*RB*, 37). We remember in particular the mysterious, baggy-trousered R. Duffill who misses the train and whose name becomes a verb, "duffilled," synonymous with being left behind; and Vassily on the Trans-Siberian Express sharing bottles of champagne with Theroux on Christmas Day.

Theroux seems most fascinated with India and most outraged with what Americans did to Vietnam. India appalls him with its "migration of ragged people" (*RB*, 119) and the sleepers in the street like some frightening population in the cities of the dead. "In India, I had decided, one could determine the sacredness of water by its degree of stagnation. The holiest was bright green . . ." (*RB*, 153).

Vietnam, on the other hand, has been abandoned to an uneasy truce: "The American mission was purely sententious and military; nowhere was there evidence of the usual municipal preoccupations of a colonizing power . . . we didn't want to stay in Vietnam, and so no vision of the country, except abstract notions of political and military order, were ever formed" (*RB*, 250, 251). Americans damaged the Vietnamese and then abandoned them. Theroux adds a postscript at the end of the chapter on Vietnam: "Now—April 1975—most of the Vietnam towns I passed through by rail have been blown up, all have been captured, and many of their people killed. For the survivors the future is melancholy, and the little train no longer runs between Hue and Danang" (*RB*, 266).

The Old Patagonian Express: By Train through the Americas (1979): "Enormous Empty Spaces"

The Old Patagonian Express is a far more self-conscious book than *The Great Railway Bazaar* but in many ways for that reason provides a deeper and more satisfying journey into the strange world without and the often stranger world within. Here Theroux formulates and describes that "lucidity of loneliness" that lies at the center of both his travel books and his fiction. And here the landscape of Patagonia embodies that central vision in its biblical, prehistoric emptiness, the "dehydrated wilderness [of] this solitary condition. . . . The Patagonian paradox was this: to be here, it helped to be a miniaturist, or else interested in enormous empty spaces. . . . You had to choose between the tiny or the vast" (*PE,* 403). In this "perfectly quiet" and "odorless" desert Theroux discovers that *"Nowhere is a place."* And his attention to detail, his focus on the "tiny," reveals his entire method. His disciplined scrutiny of the detail saves him—and the reader—from "enormous empty spaces."

Theroux's journey this time is far from comfortable. He encounters long delays, volcanic landscapes, thick jungles, the labyrinth of trying to buy tickets and discover timetables, and experiences long bouts of altitude sickness and homesickness. Still he remembers that he has set off from a cold, wintry Boston in the winter of 1978 and evaded the record-breaking blizzard that engulfed that city in February: "I had boarded the Lake Shore Limited in South Station, and after a few snowy days I had been rattling under clear skies to Mexico. I had not been robbed or fallen seriously ill. . . . I felt certain that I would make it to Esquel in Patagonia, the small town I had seen on my map that had become an arbitrary destination" (*PE,* 337). And there is that sense of elated escape, having "just finished a novel [*Picture Palace*] which had meant "two years of indoor activity" (*PE,* 6). He hopes that his "vagrant mood" will continue to see him through.

Theroux sizes up the countries, the places, and the people he encounters and passes through from Mexico's squalid xenophobia and nostalgia to Argentina's insular philistinism and fertility. Machu Picchu comes as a revelation beyond the sacred Incan valley in Peru: "It sprawled across the peak, like a vast broken skeleton picked clean by condors. For once, the tourists were silent" (*PE,* 318). And so is Theroux, who knows when to hold his tongue and let this last image at the end of a chapter linger in the reader's imagination. In hushed, almost reverent tones he reports his conversations about literature and language with the Argentinian novelist, Jorge Luis Borges: "What I saw was close to angelic. . . . His was the perfect face for a sage . . . he could look like a clown, but never a fool.

He was the gentlest of men; there was no violence in his talk and none in his gestures" (*PE,* 374, 375).

Theroux develops certain themes throughout the book. He is very aware of old colonialist traditions and routines, discovering them in immaculate working order in the Canal Zone and in Colon with "the tenements of the poor on one side of the tracks. . . . and the military symmetries of the imperial buildings on the other side" (*PE,* 225). He's appalled by the poverty he comes upon: "these poor places accumulate, until you pray for something different, a little hope to give them hope. To see a country's poverty is not to see into its heart, but it is very hard to look beyond such pitiable things" (*PE,* 153). And his indignation boils over at the hordes of homeless children curling up in doorways to keep warm and the Indians reduced to beasts of burden, owned by landowners, "always aliens in their own country" (*PE,* 297).

Visions of hell permeate the book: a soccer game in El Salvador suggests "a form of gang warfare" (*PE,* 135). Outside the stadium mobs riot and overturn cars; "the color was infernal, yellow dust sifted and whirled among craterlike pits, small cars with demonic headlights moved slowly from hole to hole like mechanical devils" (*PE,* 141). In 1969 El Salvador and Honduras actually fought a war, erupting from a soccer game. At the stadium "the scene was like one of those lurid murals of hell you see in Latin American churches" (*PE,* 141); and in order to emphasize this image, Theroux describes a painting of hell in a church in Quito, Ecuador, as "an accurate representation of a nighttime football game in El Salvador" (*PE,* 274).

The landscape of suffering appalls Theroux. He lunges verbally at some complacent tourists: "The churches here have bloodier Christs . . . life is bloodier here, isn't it? In order to believe that Christ suffered you have to know that he suffered more than you. . . . These divine figures . . . had to seem braver, more tortured, richer, or bloodier in order to seem blessed" (*PE,* 316, 317).

Theroux attempts to grasp Spanish America as a whole and describe it. In this he is both perceptive and a victim of his own northern culture. From the Texas border he conjures up "the featureless, night-haunted republics of Latin America" (*PE,* 40). The city of Nuevo Laredo, across the border from Laredo, Texas, suggests "all of Latin America [with its] brothels and basket factories"; the border, almost Manichean in its division of cultures, demonstrates "the relationship between the puritanical efficiency north of [it] and the bumbling and passionate disorder—the anarchy of sex and hunger—south of it" (*PE,* 41–2). Governments remain "bureaucratic and crooked, unstable, fickle, and barbarous" (*PE,* 142). Central America is "haywire; it was as if New England had gone completely to ruin, and places like Rhode Island and Connecticut were run by maniacal generals and thuggish policemen" (*PE,* 147). The landscape reels from "riots, civil wars, and revolutions, but also the uproarious earthquakes and incessant vulcanisms" (*PE,* 97). No wonder every national emblem displays a volcano.

Theroux always reads as he travels, commenting on the authors, but it is Edgar Allan Poe's *Narrative of Arthur Gordon Pym* that most influences his own narrative here. He finds it terrifying; "the book was an experience of pure terror . . . it was a nightmare journey, and it produced nightmares in me" (*PE,* 192). He reads *Pym* to Borges; it is one of Borges's favorite books: " 'Time for Poe,' he said. 'Please take a seat' " (*PE,* 369). The plot strangles Theroux in its "hangman's noose" (*PE,* 215), and a tourist's tale of a hurricane terrifies "like a page of *Arthur Gordon Pym*" (*PE,* 313). Theroux's terror of the empty space, the darker side of Patagonia's magnificent emptiness and the horrors associated with the encapsulated self, culminates in that journey high in the mountains of Colombia, where he experiences "only a gray sea kingdom of mist, like the horror scene that greets Arthur Pym at the end of his voyage . . . my senses in collapse" (*PE,* 257).

It is that darker vision of the self, reflected in Theroux's grimmer journey through Spanish America, that finally emerges in *The Old Patagonian Express,* making it a far more self-conscious, less self-assured vision than the exuberant "innocence" of *The Great Railway Bazaar.* This accounts for the greater depth and more thought-provoking content of what stands at this point in his career as Theroux's masterpiece of travel.

The Kingdom by the Sea: A Journey around Great Britain (1983): "Fragile and breakable and easily poisoned"

At the very end of *The Kingdom by the Sea,* after describing "that dirty and desecrated look that I thought of as English" (*KS,* 350) at Southend on the coast, the last stop of his journey around Britain,

Theroux explains almost with regret "that a country could sound sad if you spoke the language" (*KS*, 353). A tone of sadness and the theme of desecration and decay permeate this third travel book, as Theroux conjures up a grim, postindustrial future and seems to plod from coastal town to coastal town, approving some, denigrating most. As Theroux insists, "I wanted to examine the particularities of the present" (*KS*, 9), an admirable notion he often links too easily with another intention: "I cultivated complainers" (*KS*, 71).

The Kingdom by the Sea describes no romantic journey, and Theroux states very clearly what his book will *not* be: "There is an English dream of a warm summer evening on a branch-line train. Just that sentence can make an English person over forty fall silent with the memory of what has now become a golden fantasy of an idealized England: the comfortable dusty coaches rolling through the low woods; the sun gilding the green leaves and striking through the carriage windows . . . birdsong . . . the mingled smells of fresh grass and coal smoke; and the expectations of being met by someone very dear on the platform of a country station" (*KS*, 311). What Theroux sees is a country gone to seed, where the very old huddle along the coast and stare out at the sea: "It seemed to me to hold the possibility of the ultimate fright, an experience of nothingness. . . . These people were looking in the direction of death" (*KS*, 35, 81). Towns look "elderly and respectable and cliffy . . . in a tawdry-genteel way" (*KS*, 247): empty hotels and rooming houses offer no comfort; ugly shallys and caravans (British names for trailers) clutter the landscape; firing ranges, power stations, and sewage farms block the sight of the sea and dominate the edge of land; unemployment has become the norm; and Butlin's Holiday Camps proliferate and imprison their desperate revelers: "The whole affair reminded me a little of Jonestown. . . . They were so ugly. . . . This, I felt, would be the English coastal town of the future . . . it was a sleazy paradise," encapsulating "the deadened imagination and the zombie-like attitude of the strolling people" (*KS*, 131–35).

Visions of a grim future predominate. The future will reveal "a sick imprisoned atmosphere" (*KS*, 307) in which "villages were becoming crabbed and shrunken, and businesses were closing . . . the urban areas were growing in population and becoming poorer" (*KS*, 300). "It struck me that as time passed some countries with nothing in common but poverty would begin to resemble one another . . . everyone's junk is just the same" (*KS*, 41). Everywhere Theroux sees "this postindustrial slump, with little hope of recovery. . . . [There is only] the great silence . . . there was no work. Industry had come and gone" (*KS*, 198). And in this grim vision of the future there will be only wilderness, "in which most people lived hand to mouth, and the rich would live like princes. . . . All the technology would serve the rich" (*KS*, 44). Cities like those in Northern Ireland would contain a Control Zone, the center cordoned off with exits and entrances; "inside the Control Zone life was fairly peaceful and the buildings generally undamaged. . . . It was not hard to imagine Manhattan Island as one large Control Zone. . . . Ulster suggested to me the likely eventuality of sealed cities in the future" (*KS*, 235).

Such a vision tends to overpower Theroux's eye and seems less a product of his journey than a culmination of some prior thinking and feeling. One is not sure which came first, the vision of the future or the journey around the coast. He still describes the landscape and sizes up the people as imagistically and succinctly as we have come to expect. In Barrow he even manages to look up Richard Cuthbert Duffill, the "Mr. Duffill" who was "abandoned by one's own train" and lent his name to the verb to suggest just that, "duffilled," in *The Great Railway Bazaar*. Duffill has died, but Theroux finds his sister-in-law and learns his strange biography, a life which convinces Theroux "that he had almost certainly been a spy" (*KS*, 327). And his descriptions of Northern Ireland, along with his eloquent obeisance to Cape Wrath, the northwestern tip of Scotland, provide dramatic chapters in the book. But the futuristic grimness hangs like a gloomy shroud around the whole.

Theroux's trip took place in the spring and summer of 1982, and he charts the public events of the times. The Pope's visit, the railway strike, the birth of Prince William, and the mad murderer loose in Yorkshire pop up throughout his journey, but the biggest event is, of course, the Falklands War with Argentina, what Borges described as "like two bald men fighting over a comb" (*KS*, 39). Theroux juxtaposes the escalation of the war with the ordinary people and events he encounters. The day he reaches Northern Ireland, spotting "the sunlit ghost towns of the Ulster coast . . . the British army entered Port Stanley, forcing the Argentines to surrender. The next morning's newspapers all had the same headline: VICTORY!" (*KS*, 242). Thus is born "the Falklands' spirit" at a time when Theroux describes the British way of dealing with the railway strike: "Inaction was a form of coping" (KS, 330). The ironies, effortlessly presented, may also be much too facile.

Having lived in London since 1971, Theroux has eyed the British long enough to sum them up carefully and fairly. He describes the queen and her prince as "decent philistines," representing "a middle-class monarchy" (KS, 297). London suggests a smug independent republic. The long list of things he finds odd about the British from wallpapering their ceilings to sunbathing in their underwear, he balances with the things about them he likes from "the bread, the fish, the cheese" to "the trains and the modesty and truthfulness of people" (KS, 290). They are law-abiding people, and they reveal a "habitual patience that stiffened the English like a kind of hard glaze," despite the stoic despair and inertia (KS, 122).

In Ireland Theroux explores a war-torn land. He constantly asks how Catholics differ from Protestants and is told that "a Catholic's eyes are closer together" (KS, 215), "the Protestants are from Scottish stock" (KS, 218), and "it was the way a Protestant talked; he was better educated" (KS, 221). Rain engulfs him, and desolation surrounds him. He discovers "a sort of cult of death in Ulster" (KS, 232) and defines the "ultimate horror" as "bombs, murders, peoples' hands being hacksawed off, or men having their kneecaps shot off as a punishment for disloyalty, or the tar-and-feathering of young girls socializing with soldiers . . . it was unbearable" (KS, 237). Amid Ulster's "nightmare charm" and "moldering buildings" he designs his own theories based on Irish men and women, the one prone to dereliction, the other to duty: "Irish Catholicism was one long litany of mother imagery and mother worship, which only bolstered the odd family pattern," the mother as breadwinner (KS, 228). "The men had no responsibilities. . . . It was idleness as much as religion that made Ulstermen fighting mad" (KS, 228). War erupts in such a static society, the children "got destruction in their heads" (KS, 245), and with everyone believing in an afterlife, the present horror continues.

Theroux is most drawn to Scotland. The "elemental" coastline with its naked steepness strikes him as "the most spectacular coastline I had seen so far in Britain—huger than Cornwall, darker than Wales, wilder than Antrim" (KS, 260). It may be the equivalent of the Scottish self-reliance he so much admires—and sees in himself. And he waxes rhapsodic about Cape Wrath. For him the Cape is "unimaginable . . . I felt I had penetrated a fastness of mountains and moors. . . . I had found something new" (*KS,* 275). Like the desert emptiness of Patagonia, Cape Wrath stuns him with its eeriness: "It was not picturesque and it was practically unphotographable. It was stunningly empty. It looked like a corner of another planet, and at times it seemed diabolical. . . . It was like a world apart, an unknown place in this the best-known country in the world. No sooner had I left it than I wanted to go back" (*KS,* 277, 282).

Perhaps the gloomy grimness of this book arises from Theroux's blurred and uncertain images and ideas about what exactly the coast should represent. On the one hand he feels that "a country tended to seep to its coast: it was concentrated there. . . . People naturally gravitated to the coast" (*KS,* 5), and nowhere in England was more than sixty-five miles from the sea. On the other hand "the coast was where you got rid of things" (*KS,* 159). Nuclear power stations and sewage farms "were shoved onto the coast." The initial description suggests that the coast clearly represents the country it surrounds. The second suggests that the coast is a dumping grounds for the worst things the country wishes to get rid of. If the second image is correct, then Theroux's using the coast to conjure up a grim future will not stand up; if the first is true, more than likely it will. Theroux never quite resolves this dilemma.

The deranged coast remains a poisoned shore, whether it has "floated from the darker interior of England," the place where "a century of pulverized civilization had been deposited" (*KS,* 140), or whether its very nature as a coastline makes it "fragile and breakable and easily poisoned" (*KS,* 172). In any case Theroux in scrutinizing "the peculiarities of the present" creates a vision that cannot compete with the great railway bazaar or with the Spanish-American hell; the details don't quite prove the point. We are left with the decay and the erosion and the notion that somehow it is the key to a miserable universal future.

Theroux's latest travel books, *Sailing through China* (1983) and *The Imperial Way: By Rail from Peshawar to Chittagong* (1985), serve as only minor and almost incidental additions to his work. They, too, are filled with eloquent perceptions and striking details but because they are so short lack the sweep and vision of his three earlier travel books.

Theroux realizes that "a travel book can be literature, but . . .

the form itself has fatal insufficiencies. And one of them is, 'Why this occasion for this thing you are writing?' A novel is formed by an imaginative impulse, and it usually justifies itself in every line."[11] In *The Great Railway Bazaar* he also realized that "travel writing, which cannot but be droll at the outset, moves from journalism to fiction" (*RB*, 297). We catch glimpses and hints of what will become the novel *The Mosquito Coast* (1982) in *The Old Patagonian Express* and the short story "The Autumn Dog" in *The Consul's File* (1977) in *The Great Railway Bazaar*. Nameless fugitives in Vietnam become "a fictional possibility, a situation containing both a riddle and some clues for solving it" (*RB*, 248), a prelude to the novel, *The Family Arsenal* (1976). The way is clear: "The difference between travel writing and fiction is the difference between recording what the eye sees and discovering what the imagination knows. Fiction is pure joy" (*RB*, 341). What Theroux's imagination knows is for us to discover in his fiction.

Chapter Four
The Short Stories: "I'm This Other Person"

In discussing his third volume of short stories, *World's End and Other Stories* (1982), Theroux explained, "There are little connections between them, but that doesn't make a novel."[1] There are little, and often large, connections between many of the stories in Theroux's four collections. He seems interested in producing stories that interlock and comment on one another, as if several stories suggest different facets of a similar theme or outlook.

His first collection, *Sinning with Annie and Other Stories* (1972), is his thinnest in terms of connections within the volume, but several tales do involve exotic settings and cultural clashes, the kind associated with Theroux's early African and Malaysian years and his early novels. By the time he collected the stories in *World's End* the connections are many and various, including structural and thematic similarities along with the juxtaposition of characters and incidents. The most obvious connections appear in *The Consul's File* (1977) and *The London Embassy* (1983) in which the stories are narrated and seemingly collected by the American consul, Spencer Monroe Savage. His point of view and personality connect the various tales, as do the repetition of certain characters, the interlocking of certain plots, and the creation of a specific social milieu which permeates the whole.

Most of Theroux's tales present an encounter between two strong-willed people, as if the short story form were itself a kind of conversation or re-creation of a social confrontation. "The short story is often a piece of mimicry," Theroux has said, "or like ventriloquism, it's assuming another voice, another posture; that's the fun of it, actually. You can just project or extend your mind and say, 'I'm this other person.' "[2]

Theroux's tone remains brisk, swift, dry-eyed, and self-assured. He distances himself from his characters in order to report on them, line by line, preserving his ironies for the discrepancies between

what they think they are doing or saying and what they actually
do and say. He can be abrupt and succinct in reporting their personalities and eccentricities. They may harbor myths and romantic
notions; he does not. As Malcolm Cowley wrote about *World's End:*
"They are brisk, cruel, how-we-poor-bastards-live-today stories and
I admired them with tremors."[3] The "cruelty" lies in the careful
and deliberate realism of Theroux's lines, each a kind of indictment
about the particular character or culture, honing in on what he
considers to be the truth of the matter despite his characters' or a
culture's presumptions.

Theroux has written, "My real weakness is for a well-made ghost
story. . . . I do like M. R. James very much. . . . I like Poe."[4]
Several of his tales fall into Poe's territory with their Gothic horrors
and evil spirits. And his few detective stories suggest Poe's tales of
ratiocination as well. A penchant for the surprise ending, the sudden
twist of fate, suggests Poe, too, but may also come with the territory
of the tale since its incarnation at the hands of O. Henry. Two long
children's stories, published separately, *A Christmas Card* (1978) and
London Snow: A Christmas Story (1979), reveal his interest in conjuring up ghostly tales.

Sinning with Annie and Other Stories (1972)

Theroux collected fourteen stories he'd written during his stay in
Singapore from 1968 to 1971 to produce his first volume of short
stories. Many of them are set in "alien" places such as India, Dar
es Salaam in Tanganyika, Russia, Malaysia, Singapore, and Surabaya
and some others closer to home in Boston, Maine, and Amherst.
The subjects include lust, death, divorce, attempted murder, suicide, manipulations and betrayals of all kinds, often appearing in
the guise of cultural clashes: the American in Russia, the Indian in
Boston, old Dutch Jews in Surabaya, the American in Czechoslovakia. In most of them marriages fail: "[M]arriage had increased
his loneliness by violating his reveries."[5] In "Dog Days" Len Rowley
lusts after the Chinese housekeeper, who eventually blackmails him
and gets the upper hand. Ambrose McCloud tries to murder his
nervous, complaining wife in the bathtub in "You Make Me Mad."
In "Hayseed" the philandering Wilbur returns from a trip to Ban-
gor, Maine, to his hometown to find that his wife Lavinia has hanged
herself. The Grigsons use their friend Leo Mockler to engineer their

divorce in "What Have You Done to Our Leo?" Only the Russian invasion of Czechoslovakia salvages the rocky relationship between Morris Rosetree and his Czech wife, Lepska Kanek, in "A Political Romance." And Harry and his wife battle over their friends the Crowleys in "A Deed Without a Name," a tale told in the wife's querulous manner with her paranoid sense of insult and betrayal: "If I do not know the name of what they did to us it is not because there is none" (*SA,* 166).

In "Memories of a Curfew," which surfaces again in *Sunrise with Seamonsters* as "Scenes from a Curfew" (suggesting perhaps its importance or interest for the author) Theroux spins an autobiographical yarn about swapping girl friends with another friend. At first it is fun: "our clothes slung over our shoulders . . . At the time I thought it was a monstrous game . . . played to kill time and defeat fear and loneliness—something the curfew demanded . . . [But] I had not been playing; all my gestures had been scared and serious. I stopped trusting . . . And so I left Africa" (*SA,* 116). That loss of trust permeates the stories in *Sinning with Annie.*

The tales reveal encounters and confrontations of all kinds, the sort of doubling Theroux delights in. The prison warden Goldpork exacts a confession from a jailed old party member in "The Prison Diary of Jack Faust." Faust's apparent innocence slowly curdles into guilt: "My imagined innocence weighed on me and made me lax; but, guilty, I have a place—I belong" (*SA,* 18). In "A Real Russian Ikon" the American, Fred Hagberg, manages to buy an icon in Moscow from an old lady who suddenly dies, leaving him with the idea of smuggling the icon out of the country in a casket, a confrontation between personal gain and sudden death. The Indian Danny (Daneeda Schum) stalks the beautiful Indo-American girl Dorothy in "A Love Knot," only to miss her entirely. Glassman faces down the old Dutch Jews at Abe Sassoon's funeral in "A Burial at Surabaya," and Ira Hubbel, the apparent "hayseed" gas station attendant in "Hayseed," shows up Warren Root for what he really is.

Theroux has the most fun with encounters here in "Biographical Notes for Four American Poets," as he takes after four poets at an English department seminar at Amherst College, each assuming the mantle and posing as another, greater poet. Thus Denton Fuller cultivates the image of Robert Frost, Wilbur Parsons admires Wallace Stevens's discipline, Sumner Bean displays touches of Robert

Lowell and e.e. cummings, and cynical Stanley Gold, who loves to shout "love lyrics scattered with references to elimination" (*SA*, 130), wears the mantle of the New York alienated Jewish rebel.

As we have come to expect, Theroux zeroes in on the telling detail. As Danny Schum describes his method in coming to Boston from Madras, "I wanted to discover the place slowly, as one does a painting in a museum, approaching it from a great distance and picking out details as one draws nearer for the close, final dazzle" (*SA*, 64–5). He does so and discovers a typically Therouxvian dilemma: "all the anticipated details of my previous fantasy had been replaced by the actual details—unanticipated but now appropriate—of what I saw. . . . It was still fantasy, but substantiated by enough reality to make me patient in my errand" (*SA*, 67). Not many of Theroux's characters are so patient, but Danny's method parallels Theroux's own.

Theroux's less successful stories are usually too thin. The encounter evaporates, either because it is not sharply focused enough or because the characters seem mere wisps that remain undeveloped and unsubstantiated. The best stories in this volume reveal a complexity of technique, method, and subject. These include, in no particular order, "The Prison Diary of Jack Faust," "A Love Knot," "A Burial at Surabaya," and the title story, "Sinning with Annie."

"The Prison Diary of Jack Faust" begins with an apparently straightforward narrator's revealing "a valuable smuggled manuscript" (*SA*, 1) in his possession. He remarks on his years " in real prisons" (*SA*, 1), as if he were some freedom fighter recently escaped from the Russian gulag and mumbles once in a television show that "[b]eing a member of the Party was for me like being in prison" (*SA*, 1). He objects to his having "been made out to be a perfectly horrible old menace" (*SA*, 2) and sees his duty in making the manuscript public, a prison diary written by one Jack Faust somewhere in Eastern Europe. Faust's name is an alias: "It is intentionally symbolic: a *jack* is used to hoist a heavy object; he is *Jack*, the object a weighty truth he was too simple to grasp wholly" (*SA*, 6).

The diary, date by date, replaces the narrator's introduction at this point. Jack Faust—and of course his pact with the Devil reverberates in his last name—was arrested and imprisoned. The warder was named Goldpork; he and Faust "were in the Youth Wing together" (*SA*, 8) years ago. Faust writes a list of suggestions for Goldpork, "itemizing a clean-up and renovation memorandum" (*SA*, 9), but decides not to send it. He cannot understand why he has been arrested. He has been a loyal Party man: "What this country needs is a good solid overhaul by some merciless but farsighted Party man" (*SA*, 13). Goldpork turns out ironically to be that very man and the narrator of the story. Faust complains to him in person in prison, but Goldpork only reminds him of his past sins. Faust concludes: "I am not Party material, and it is clear that Goldpork is" (*SA*, 18).

Goldpork concludes his story, explaining how Faust handed over his diary, confessed, and was hanged: "It is a pity he did not live long enough to see that [my deal] at least had a reasonably happy ending" (*SA*, 19). The party purge is complete. Goldpork has exacted his revenge and has triumphed. His Faustian deal has been to extort Faust's confession from him and, thus, establish Goldpork's ascendency and victory. Betrayal triumphs and is part of the system, and Theroux's tale, divided between diary and interpreter, reveals that betrayal in his splintered and carefully engineered text. Straight narration surrounds the diary, as Goldpork has cleverly imprisoned Faust and overcome the threat he poses. The deal is complete.

"A Love Knot" is a taut tale of pursuit. Daneeda "Danny" Schum, raised by his Indian mother in Calcutta as Hindu, wishes to escape from India. After his mother dies he finds a love knot made of gold in an envelope addressed to George Chowdree, 22 Walnut Street, Boston, Massachusetts. He obtains a scholarship to a university in a Boston suburb and sails from Madras.

Danny's mixed identity and his being a stranger in a new city, "the city of quaintness and crime" (*SA*, 59), as he describes it from reading about it in novels, adds to his sensation of displacement and isolation. He pays obeisance to the stranger's eye: "Persons of mixed identity like me find it simpler to agree with the stranger's assessment. I am what other people take me for; I never challenge their assumptions" (*SA*, 63). He can retreat to the refuge of the other's presumptions. He manages to combat this sense of a kind of self-effacing silence by observing himself as a creature in some great melodramatic vision. He has read Conrad's *The Secret Agent* and thinks "Verlock could have managed his seedy shop on Charles Street" (*SA*, 64). He superimposes an actor's face on his visions of what George Chowdree must look like. And he enjoys the melodrama of his slowly picking out the details of the city and Walnut

Street, "my dead mother's piece of ornate jewelry always in my pocket, my cleverly obtained scholarship, my search, my wanderings . . . striking poses as if I was being watched" (*SA*, 66). His entire self-conscious pursuit of discovering the truth of Walnut Street smacks of "the Indian film which is filled with such paraphernalia" (*SA*, 66), a romantic melodrama he chooses to inhabit and create.

A second fantasy comes to replace the first, for in the window of the Chowdree house on Walnut Street he spies the face of an Indian girl: "I fancied that the shadow I cast in that late summer reverie was like this girl, dark and altering in rippling angles as I walked on uneven ground, a foreshortened reflection of my own personality, changeable and intriguing, joined at my foot sole" (*SA*, 67). Theroux's love of doubling extends to Danny's self-extended fantasy of himself: the die is cast. He follows the girl, sees her steal a library book, and discovers that her name is Dorothy. Discovering what books she likes to read in the library, he slips the love knot into one of them, having discovered that she is the organizer of a dance at the Biltmore for the Spring Weekend. At the dance he sees her wearing the knot on a chain around her neck. He approaches her, notices the jewel, strikes up a conversation, and they dance. Dorothy, however, announces, "I'm leaving for India the day after tomorrow. I can hardly wait" (*SA*, 75).

Danny remembers a child in Calcutta drawing figure eights in the dust, having "left a line curving at an angle in the dust, the open hourglass of an imperfect eight" (*SA*, 76). Symmetry collapses; the boy and girl move in opposite directions; each escapes to where the other will escape to or has escaped from. The love knot ironically suggests only separation and defeat.

"A Burial at Surabaya" lingers in the mind because of Theroux's descriptions of death and decay and his depiction of life lived on the margins of history in the realm of dessicated expatriates. Pallbearers resemble "eleven black crows marching with a box through the heat" (*SA*, 201). The cemetery reveals "this baking plain . . . a few acres of stony rubble signifying a dead story of habitation, which people visit to photograph" (*SA*, 202). It is "in that intermediate stage of decay that characterized the whole place, a crack through a name, a date effaced . . . a dumping ground in an old country . . . " (*SA*, 203). Such an atmosphere surrounds and nearly suffocates the old Dutch Jews burying one of their own, who regard the funeral as a chore, a dead ritual. "Why should death make someone your brother?" (*SA,* 199) asks the middle-aged, exhausted narrator, remembering Tjimahi, the concentration camp in west Java, where he knew Abe Sassoon, the deceased.

The ceremony is interrupted by a cousin Glassman, who is appalled that the funeral has begun without him and by the supposed careless mockery of the assembled friends: "Shame on you. . . . what kind of people are you?" (*SA,* 210) The narrator wonders: "What did he expect? Javanese *babus* in shiny silk pajamas holding umbrellas over our heads, a gilded coffin, the hot air split by mourners' shrieks, a wise old rabbi chanting into his nest of beard . . . ?" (*SA,* 208)

What Glassman clearly wants involves the old Jewish traditions, the ancient ceremonies of faith, not the simplistic clichés of someday joining "our brother" and intoning dully, "We should be glad he is at peace" (*SA,* 209). The narrator doesn't understand: "He went on in this vein . . . accusing us of savagery" (*SA,* 210). When Glassman leaves at last, the narrator seals his own fate, unaware of what he has revealed about himself and the old Dutch Jews: "The rest of us stayed just where we were, and no one said that young man's name again" (*SA,* 210). They return to their expatriated living death, worn out and dispirited, their values and sense of self as worn away as their traditions and as the landscape that surrounds them.

Lust powers the narrator, Arthur Viswalingam, in "Sinning with Annie," a lust so all-consuming it becomes the primal urge itself and "is in actual fact closer to anger than to gluttony . . . one is aroused quickly to both anger and lust. . . . It is possible to allay one's anger in private; lust involves other people and I believe because it does so, is the greater corruption . . . where lust is concerned, darkness is just around the corner" (*SA,* 55, 56). Arthur at thirteen has been the victim of an arranged marriage, having married Ananda, age eleven, in the Laxshminarayan Temple in the spring of 1898. The marriage was arranged by his father, a prince whose "credit had run out at last" (*SA,* 47). Neither child had any idea of what should happen on the wedding night: "At my age I could not be expected to have any idea of female nakedness. . . . You never saw anyone so young bunged into marriage as I was" (*SA,* 52, 53).

Slowly, however, against Viswalingam's will, there appeared "a little animal, a nasty little beast like the sort we worshiped" (*SA,*

52). This animal Arthur connects to his own childhood Hindu religion: "We Hindus have a curious faith that, in a manner of speaking, transforms a farmyard into a place of worship" (*SA*, 47). The animal, of course, is lust and leads to sexual shenanigans that become "fierce, fumbling and unsatisfying" (*SA*, 52). Young Arthur cannot at first figure out what to do: "I married *and* burned. This went on for many months" (*SA*, 53). But finally lust wins out and "knew no bounds." And Annie "grew ever more attractive, which goes to show that the devil may take many forms . . . " (*SA*, 56).

The irony of the story comes with the recognition that eighty-three-year-old Arthur is recalling the "sins" of his youth and recalling them from his new perspective: "The Savior of the faith I embraced only this year similarly stood in a temple" (*SA*, 48). At eighty-three Arthur has become a Christian, and his notions of sin and lust are the Christian convert's in league with his turning away from eighty-two years of being a Hindu. The arranged marriage he now sees as the product of "our degraded culture" (*SA*, 51) and the eventual and accompanying lust as the animal product of that "farmyard" worship: "The villagers worshiped a whole zoo of beasts, a pseudospiritual menagerie. . . . To be human was a crime against everyone; it was grotesque" (*SA*, 47). Thus his narration is peppered with Christian references—St. Paul's marrying and burning—and with his newfound image of himself, suggesting Eliot's dessicated Christian persona: "I am an old man in a wet month" (*SA*, 45). From his new perspective, he admits, "To be frank, I haven't the slightest idea of what goes on in the Asian mind" (*SA*, 50), a notion Theroux suggests in several other tales in this collection, conjuring up "a close glimpse into the mind of Asia" (*SA*, 176) in "Dog Days" and referring to Indians as "fabulous creatures" (*SA*, 85) in "What Have You Done to Our Leo?"

Arthur Viswalingam's newfound Christianity frightens the reader but not the convert. Arthur leads the British "to the flea pots and flesh pits, the drink shops and temples and, in a bloody crusade, we crushed the life out of the verminous population. This accomplished, we peopled the country anew, cleanly, without mess, with colder holy folk from frozen places" (*SA*, 57). Colder, indeed, with the long-thwarted vengeance of the puritan. He even admits he would have strangled Annie in these "frozen" fits, although if she had entered his room, "I would fall before her and touch my lips to her instep as if she were the Queen of Heaven" (*SA*, 57). Lust remains his god, even though his new religion despises it.

Theroux suggests how Christian conversion may disrupt and strangle an alien culture, how the West tries to overwhelm and overcome the East, and in doing so how one can be left torn apart and angry, nursing his own vengeance in place of a livelier, more sensual kind of revelry, the labyrinthine arousals of lust. Arthur may reject the "heartiness" of sex, but his conversion only reveals to the reader what a terrible choice he has made or at the very least what terrible choice old age has forced him to make. He acknowledges "my sin, namely lust" (*SA*, 55) but in doing so forfeits his birthright and his life.

World's End and Other Stories (1982)

Theroux has acknowledged the thematic connections between the stories in *World's End*: "The thread is thematic; it's the simple one of people being abroad in a metaphorical way as well as in a real way. I wanted to call the book *Overseas*, or *Abroad*. I wanted that sense of otherness of place in it." And that theme usually involves the recognition of replacing one's fantasies with a starker truth: "These people end up having to face the fact that there is no fantasy and they're going to have to come to terms with this letdown and perhaps live there and make a few compromises, and so they do."[6] The refrain is heard several times in this volume: "This was no romance . . . there was no romance" (*WE*, 155, 172).

Several characters in *World's End* seek islands of illusion, that "otherness of place" where they will be safe. In the title story, for example, Robarge, who has transplanted his family "to a bizarrely named but buried-alive district called World's End in London" (*WE*, 11), sees his house there as a "refuge" and feels certain that "[h]e had not merely moved his family but rescued them" (*WE*, 12). When he discovers that his wife is having an affair and uses their son Richard to spy on her, the sanctuary crumbles. Richard, aged six, who has revealed the affair while flying a kite with his father, refuses to comply with this assignment—" 'Mummy doesn't have a friend,' and Robarge knew he had lost the child" (*WE*, 23)—and to Robarge the house now seems "to be made of iron . . . He was saddened by the thought that he was so far from home. The darkness

hid him and hid the country . . . the darkness concealed his loss
. . . and he knew now they were all lost" (*WE,* 24).

The name, World's End, proves both prophetic in terms of the
individual tale and suggestive of the theme of the "otherness of
place" throughout the volume. Theroux has described the tale as
"a story about things closing up" and views Robarge's use of his
child as "a grave mistake . . . The child is treated as a love object,
as a possession, as a kind of mainstay, as the proof of his own right
decision. He represents too much to the man. We *do* tend to use
and misuse the people we love." Burdened by his fantasy of refuge,
Robarge enlists his son to assure him that the sanctuary is safe, and
by asking the child to spy on his mother, according to Theroux,
"his worst mistake is corrupting the child with this lie."[7] Loss and
deceit become all but inevitable with the end of the world.

In "The Greenest Island," the last story in the collection, Duval,
nineteen, and Paula, twenty-one, settle upon Puerto Rico as a place
to escape to, now that she is pregnant, and they aren't married.
Puerto Rico suggests the exotic, the greenest island, but in reality
it is poor, ruined, and shabby with "a kind of yellow decay lurking
in the color" (*WE,* 172). Green, emblematic of growth and hope,
reveals only "the late-summer tinge of yellow exhaustion. . . .
This green disfigured place was the world. . . . There was no
romance—they had brought none. It was green, that was all" (*WE,*
202, 177, 172). They long for rescue, for deliverance, and "they
craved protection. They were waiting for everything to change, and
yet nothing had changed" (*WE,* 184).

Inevitably the couple run out of money. Duval gets a job at The
Beachcomber, a new restaurant at the Hilton in San Juan. The work
is steady, but he feels trapped and uncertain: "So the salary trapped
him more completely than the fear of poverty had. The job became
central, the only important thing. . . . How easily the green island
had abstracted him and made him this new man" (*WE,* 200). Duval
meets the restaurant owner, the Beachcomber, and describes him
as "a fraud, a tycoon in old clothes, a figure of crass romance" (*WE,*
216). In a marvelously evocative scene Duval leaves the restaurant
and discovers the bloodthirsty world of the cockfight. He recoils in
horror from the cruelty and vows *"I will never get married"* (*WE,*
209).

In the end Duval abandons Paula after they have saved enough
money for the airfare home. When he walks away from his job at

the restaurant, he notices a strange light in the sky: "it was the moon behind the trees that lit them so strangely, darkening the green, like smoke beginning" (*WE,* 217). The green is darker now, more ominous, but the choice has been his to make. Within he feels his chance: "[H]e had discovered his small green soul on the island, its solitary inward conceit scribbled differently from hers, and now he could read the scribble" (*WE,* 213). He had always thought "that he was marked for some great windfall, without sacrifice" (*WE,* 173), but the sacrifice becomes necessary. A forest by the sea suggests "a kind of cowering adulthood, promising darkness, the scavenging of naked families. Alone, he could escape it" (*WE,* 188). And does.

In commenting on "The Greenest Island" Theroux explained, "I think my story is about rejecting one thing and choosing another—discovering that you're rejecting one kind of entanglement, and choosing to be a writer," a difficult but noble choice in his own life. "The Greenest Island," coming at the end of *World's End,* balances the title story: "The fellow in that story has the hope of youth. . . . That's really what I envy in the young, the fact that they have possibilities. . . . I wanted to end on the somewhat hopeful note of someone marching into the world."[8]

Robarge's iron house is somewhat relieved by Duval's greenness of soul and youth, although the darkening green and the ambiguities Theroux discovers in that color on the island, producing one of his best stories in the process (it is also his longest tale here), suggests that fantasy must always be tempered with fact, and that often trapped on the illusory island of self, "you have to work out your destiny within that small space."[9]

The "otherness of place" traps others. Professor Sheldrick in "Words Are Deeds," abandoned by his wife, runs off in Crete with an equally spiteful woman. Floyd in the hilarious "Yard Sale," who has become so "Samoa-ized" from his Peace Corps years there that he cannot abide the United States, returns to Samoa after only a few weeks at home. Miss Bristow in "Zombies," an eighty-two-year-old novelist modeled on the British novelist, Jean Rhys,[10] who dreams of death, feels like a corpse and remembers the Caribbean island of her youth. The colonial newcomer, Mr. Hand, in "The Imperial Icehouse" insists on hauling ice in a wagon across the island in the heat of the day and is slaughtered by the three black servants he forces to help him.

Two of the best encounters in the volume include Professor Lowell Bloodworth's with the exiled American poet, Walter Van Bellamy, based loosely on Robert Lowell, in "The Odd-Job Man" and that between the unnamed narrator, voraciously interested in insects, and pretentious Jerry Benda in Africa in "White Lies." Bloodworth rents a small cottage in the village of Hooke in Kent near Van Bellamy's place. He wants to publish a special edition of Van Bellamy's poems, "Introduction by Bloodworth, Notes by Bloodworth." Their meeting is a disaster, so Bloodworth puts Bellamy's odd-job man Ralph up to pilfering some of the great poet's manuscripts: " 'Listen,' said Ralph, 'make it fifty quid and I'll bring you the whole bloody lot in a bushel basket!' " (WE, 140).

Bloodworth realizes how much his ruthlessness as a critic resembles Ralph's odd jobs: "They received orders from the man whose poetry had earned him privileges, and stood at the margins of the poet's world, listening for a shout, waiting for a poem" (WE, 141). They meet in a churchyard for the transaction. Examining the scribblings later, Bloodworth is appalled, "but the drunken typing and misspelling that made them valueless to Bloodworth did not disguise the beauty of the lines" (WE, 142). Ralph has also enclosed his own poem. Back in Amherst Bloodworth proudly announces his find: "I've got some unpublished Bellamy variants in here, and the work of a new poet; he's terribly regional but quite exciting" (WE, 143). As Theroux once remarked, "During the vacations in June, all English professors turn into writers and become predatory."[11] So much for the literary world of poetry and critics!

Jerry Benda, teaching at a bush school in Africa along with the more serious and shy unnamed narrator who tells the tale, "White Lies," enjoys a sexual liaison with Ameena, an African girl he met at the Rainbow Bar. The narrator studies insects but abhors Jerry's deceitfulness: "But Jerry was so careful, his lies such modest calculations, he was always believed" (WE, 105). He conceals where in Boston he is from—Watertown, not Belmont—and, handsome and charming, he is courted by the British wives in the compound: "I had been in Africa for two years and had replaced any ideas of sexual conquest with the possibility of a great entomological discovery" (WE, 107).

The story moves with Poesque precision. Jerry stalks Petra, the headmaster's daughter. He abandons Ameena, who storms into his house one day and leaves a shirt; he later burns it. The narrator grinds his teeth, "resenting the thought that Jerry had all the luck. First Ameena, now Petra. And he had ditched Ameena" (*WE*, 113). However, Jerry fails to make it with Petra because he has discovered "a mass of tiny reddened patches, like fly bites" (*WE*, 104) all over his body, which he reveals to the narrator. Maggots breed in the boils. Jerry thinks Ameena's shirt has been bewitched. The narrator pries the maggots from the boils, "and I must admit that it gave me a certain pleasure. It was not only that Jerry deserved to suffer for his deceit . . . this was a startling discovery for me, as an entomologist. I had never seen such creatures before" (*WE*, 117). At last Jerry leaves, convinced he is suffering from "the curse of the white worm" (*WE*, 118). The narrator later discovers that the flies, shaped "like a Muslim woman's cloak," the same kind of cloak Ameena wore when she delivered the shirt, "laid their eggs on laundry." Ameena had always ironed Jerry's shirts: "Of course, laundry was always ironed—even drip-dry shirts—to kill them. Everyone who knew Africa knew that" (*WE*, 119).

"White Lies" presents Theroux at his Poesque best: the obsessed and rational narrator, the unfolding of a supposed curse, the ambiguity of the title, the carefully crafted plot driven toward its horrific climax. The style and tone reflect the other tales in *World's End* as well: the brisk, cool, acerbic one-liners with their misogynistic reverberations that size up the characters unflinchingly, perhaps accounting for Malcolm Cowley's referring to these stories as "cruel" and yet admiring them "with tremors." The characters may seek their islands of illusions, but they encounter only the fact that their fantasies cannot last. They each must deal with the collapse of those worlds, with the world's end to such romantic hopes. "World's End," "The Greenest Island," and "White Lies" all deal with that shock of recognition that lies at the heart of Theroux's fiction.

The Consul's File (1977)

The interconnections among the stories in *The Consul's File* stand out so clearly that the book seems almost like a new kind of fragmented novel. Each story can stand on its own, but each is narrated by the American Consul viewing a British or formerly British community—nameless, until the last line of *The London Embassy*—and several involve characters who appear again and again in the other collected tales. At the same time the stories take place in Ayer

Hitam, the flat dusty backwater in Malaysia to which the Consul has been sent to close up shop, and throughout the volume a full-bodied, multiracial, socially stratified society is revealed and described.

Ayer Hitam, a name which means "Black Water," reveals dust and junk. To the westerner it can be both seductive and destructive. As the consul explains in his final letter before his departure, "We crave simple societies, but they're no good for us . . . you can grow here; but after that you must go, or be destroyed. . . . Countries like this are possessed on the one hand by their own strangling foliage, and on the other by outside interests. . . . Between jungle and viability, there is nothing—just the hubbub of struggling mercenaries, native and expatriate, stalking their futile claims."[12] Oil palms are replacing the American rubber estates. "No one lived in the town, really; people just went to club meetings there" (CF, 122).

Theroux once admitted, "I have always been an admirer of Burgess—his Enderby books and The Malayan Trilogy."[13] The racial and social hierarchies and labyrinths of The Consul's File suggest Burgess's descriptions in his trilogy. Malays, loose-limbed and slender, live in neighboring kampongs outside of town. Tamils work the rubber estates or like Peeraswami serve white masters, such as the consul. The Chinese own and run the shops, decorating them with photographs of their families, a sign of ancestor worship. The Laruts, who sell butterflies, maintain a gentle demeanor and live in the jungle. Communists seem like "early Christians," members of their own "priestly cabal" (CF, 117). For British expatriates "home was defeat" (CF, 161). Here they hang on at the Club, maintain an edgy suburban exclusivity, and continue to exercise their racial prejudices, especially against the aloof and inscrutable Japanese.

Most Americans can be obnoxious and demanding, like "one of those ravished American women, grazing the parapet of middle age, with a monotonous libido and an expensive camera, vowing to have a fling at the romance travel was supposed to provide" (CF, 92). Younger Americans are numbered among "the Vietnam generation with a punished conscience and muddled notions of colonialism" (CF, 74).

The City Bar is run by Woo Boh Shee. A French-Canadian priest, Father LeFever, runs the mission. The Club, which resembles "a lost world, but not an ancient one; here it was eternally 1938" (*CF*, 16), has given up polo and taken up tennis. Its members parade a "ghastly jollity [as] a defense against strangers" (*CF*, 190), and "as usual when someone stayed away from the Club he became all the more present in conversation" (*CF*, 180). The Footlighters Drama Group meets every Wednesday evening, and its members are proud of their production of Somerset Maugham's *The Letter*. The Communists' "priestly cabal . . . had its more vulgar counterpart in the lounge of the Ayer Hitam Club" (*CF*, 117). Those left out of the Club—"Methodist Chinese, Catholic Indian, undeclared half-caste" (*CF*, 23)—the misfits, are feted each year with a Christmas party at Dr. Alec Stewart's house. Even the misfits enjoy their special rites.

Racial prejudice and social roles circumscribe the town's routines and practices. The consul is aware of "that sinking feeling you get at a national boundary or an unguarded frontier" (*CF*, 115), since Ayer Hitam is full of these. Reggie Woo, the son of Woo Boh Shee, tries to appear impeccably British, "the person who leaves his race behind, who goes to school and returns home English" (*CF*, 111), but winds up tending bar with his father. Linda Clem falls in love with a poor prince who sponges off her: "A hopeless liaison: he wanted to be American, she aimed at being Malay—the racial somersault often mistaken for tolerance. It was usually inverted bigotry, ratting on your own race" (*CF*, 48). When the liaison collapses, "she acquired the affectations of a memsahib" (*CF*, 52), the overbearing role of the white female colonialist who ranks high in the racial and social caste: "Now she was in a high-backed Malacca chair under a fan calling out, 'Boy!' " (*CF*, 52). The English maintain their "fatal attitudes" (*CF*, 103) toward the Japanese. The Japanese "had lost the war and gained the world; they were unreadable . . . it was a total absence of trust in anyone who was not Japanese . . . these [were] new men, a postwar instrument, the perfectly calibrated Japanese" (*CF*, 103).

Angela Miller, the sultan's mistress and local Footlighter, insists on playing Suzie Wong in the next production. The pushy American, Margaret Harbottle, moves in on the consul's hospitality and with her interference upsets everyone's routine: "The Malays wanted to humiliate her; the Chinese suggested turning the matter over to a secret society; the Indians had pressed for some expensive litigation. It was the first time I had seen the town united in this way"

(*CF*, 38). The would-be novelist Sundrum, who is "half-Chinese, half-Indian and so looked Malay" (*CF*, 150), belabors the stereotypical argument: "You're white—what's the difference? The world belongs to you. Who are we? Illiterates, savages! What right do we have to publish our books—you own all the printeries. You're Prospero, I'm Caliban" (*CF*, 155). In Philip Mason's *Prospero's Magic: Some Thoughts on Class and Race* the author described the "Prospero complex" as that Anglo-Saxon ideal of authority, order, and service that views all other races as inferiors, children in search of a great white father to guide and teach them.[14] That British self-image as an outmoded point of view pervades the consul's assessment of Ayer Hitam.

The consul's point of view also pervades the stories in his file. He writes in that breezy, self-assured manner we have come to recognize as part and parcel of Theroux's style, often rude, for the most part dry-eyed and tart, consistently and carefully assessing himself and his surroundings. As a bachelor he loves his freedom: "[Y]ou were married and lived in a particular house; unmarried, you lived in the world, and there were no answers required of you" (*CF*, 61). He expresses the same clear-eyed vision that we discovered in Theroux's travel books. He sees himself as "an unrepentent eavesdropper" (*CF*, 208) and glories in his essential anonymity. Details catch his eye: "Truth is not a saga of alarming episodes; it is a detail, a small clear one, that gives fiction life" (*CF*, 54). And he admires his own clear-sightedness: "It takes time to decide that your first impression, however brutal, was correct" (*CF*, 159). "We tend to see mystery in emptiness," he explains, "but I knew from Africa that emptiness is more often just that: behind it is a greater emptiness" (*CF*, 207). When he opens the previous consul's files, he discovers that there are no secrets: "[I]n fact, most of the pages were blank" (*CF*, 6). To that first impression he tenaciously clings.

And yet he realizes that his life has been too guarded, that he has never been reckless enough. He recognizes his own reticence as a kind of self-protection, a quiet form of cowardice, and he envies Sundrum's "peace of mind in this green clearing" (*CF*, 153), which proves false but which illuminates his own uncertainties. Fears stalk him. In "Dengue Fever," named for an affliction from which Theroux himself suffered, he "felt certain that [Ladysmith, the character hallucinating because of the fever] had passed that horror on" (*CF*, 82). He upbraids himself and speaks of "the danger that all of us deserved" (*CF*, 173), as if this were the new "white man's burden" in an Asian country or a necessary shock of recognition to force him out of his own complacent shell. Even his bachelor freedom is suspect: "Where is his act? Bachelorhood looks like selfish delay, and the words are loaded: bachelor means queer, spinster means hag" (*CF*, 188).

The consul may be a somewhat idealized image of the Theroux persona of the travel books, but at the same time he functions as a character in fiction. When he first arrives in Ayer Hitam, Fred Squibb, an English manager of timber estates, informs him that Alec Stewart enjoys flagellation in private. Immediately "the one fact that I had been told made me suspicious of everyone I met, and when I realized the sort of double life that people led—and had proof of it—I felt rather inadequate myself" (*CF*, 207–8). He had prided himself on his moderation, dependability, and patience and declares, "I understand the mind of the West" (*CF*, 135), but in trusting no one, because of Squibb's indiscretion, he cannot trust himself and decides, "I wasn't a character; it was the other people who mattered, not me. . . . Other people's lives are so much more interesting than one's own" (*CF*, 208). The ironic upshot of Squibb's tale, recounted in the consul's letter to a fellow American, William Ladysmith, at the conclusion of the book, is that it is Squibb who enjoys the whip, not Alec Stewart: "he'd made this all Alec's secret" (*CF*, 211).

In any case the consul decides, "feeling a little like a souvenir hunter . . . to write" (*CF*, 2). If other people are more interesting than himself, he'll pursue their tales and collect their emblematic encounters with the strange world around them. They all "thought of themselves as 'characters' . . . but there is something impersonal in the celebration of eccentricity" (*CF*, 3). What he decides to do is to "deal with the others . . . in my own way" (*CF*, 212).

Along the way he discovers that someone like Angela Miller has too many facets to her personality to capture: "Was she the person who had a nervous breakdown, the queen of the Footlighters, or the Sultan's mistress? She was all three and much more, but no story could unify those three different lives; they were not linked. The truth is too complicated for words: truth is water" (*CF*, 206). And yet he persists in "Black Water" to discover good stories, to avoid poetic justice, and to seek out the truth.

His encounter with Sundrum in "Coconut Gatherer" reveals the discrepancies between art and life. When he first perceives Sundrum as content and genuine—"And I think that if I could have traded my life for his I would have done so" (*CF,* 153)—Sundrum's book appears "mawkish, the prose appalling and artless, simply a sludge of wrongly punctuated paragraphs" (*CF,* 154). Yet when he returns to listen to a querulous and bitter Sundrum launch his racist tirades, no longer the "solitary soulful man" but "manic . . . foolish or arrogant" (*CF,* 159), he views the book differently, this time with pleasure: "I admired . . . the rough charm of his sermonizing . . . beneath the husk and fiber of his imitative lyricism so much of what he described was recognizably true to me" (*CF,* 161). Art lies and tells the truth, a lesson the consul slowly learns in his own gathering of tales and encounters, which resembles it would seem Theroux's own pursuit of writing and assessing.

The "sin" to avoid is that fatality of fiction that creates a false romance for people to imitate: "Ayer Hitam seemed tainted, and it was cursed with romance that was undetectable to anyone who was not sitting on the club verandah with a drink in his hand" (*CF,* 206). At the very beginning the consul hears stories—"The place, people said, was full of stories" (*CF,* 2)—but one of them "I later read in a volume of Somerset Maugham in the club library" (*CF,* 2). The "villain" of romance turns out to be Maugham, as characters in Ayer Hitam try to pattern themselves after the creatures in his fictions. The consul lets Maugham have it and in doing so further reveals the central landscape of Theroux's post-colonial fiction: "What tedious eccentricity Maugham was responsible for! He made heroes of these time-servers; he glorifed them by being selective and leaving out their essential flaws. He gave people like Squibb destructive models to emulate, and he encouraged expatriates to pity themselves. It is the essence of the romantic lie" (*CF,* 205–6).

The consul views the very notion of describing one's self as an odd character as Maugham's corrosively romantic legacy. "Buffles," the selfishly, self-indulgent sultan, models himself on Maugham's snobbish British products. Gillespie, the "last colonial" and planter, who has stayed on too long and is murdered, the consul describes as "another Maugham hero whose time was up" (*CF,* 172), as if he died of old fictional myths instead of Communist bullets.

Romance has tainted the language: "Their locutions were tropical: any sickness was a fever, diarrhea was dysentery, every rainfall a monsoon. It wasn't romance, it was habit" (*CF,* 4). Flint, the number two man in the American Embassy in Kuala Lumpur, laments, "I remember when an overseas post meant some excitement. Hard work, drinking, romance, a little bit of the Empire," to which the consul responds, "The White Man's Burden" (*CF*, 8). "That's my favorite poem," Flint replies. At the annual Christmas party for the misfits in "White Christmas," people recall English Christmases or conjure them up. The consul describes them "like children with old inaccurate memories, preparing themselves for something that would never occur" (*CF*, 27) and records Sundrum's remark that "white is the Chinese color for death" (*CF*, 28). "The deceits of the East" (CF, 49) may provide "a little mystery [which] is often easier to bear than an unwelcome fact" (*CF*, 201), but the consul sees his role as observer as bearing down on such nostalgic falsehoods and eradicating them once and for all. Of course from his perspective he conjures up a kind of bitter romance of his own but finds it a necessary elixir to awaken us—and himself?—from "the essence of the romantic lie" (*CF*, 206) and the exaggerated self-pity of willful expatriates.

Of the twenty stories in *The Consul's File*, nine deal with some odd character involving himself or herself in the affairs of Ayer Hitam; five—the first three and the concluding two—concern the consul's arrival, introduction to "Black Water," and departure; three others reveal Theroux's Poesque love of the ghost tale and the horror of strange fevers, strange hallucinations, and stranger transformations initiated by witch doctors; two suggest Poe's tales of ratiocination; and one involves a bittersweet romance, the results of a collapsing marriage of the kind that haunts the entire volume. "Married people argue about everything—anything" (*CF*, 41), Strang quips in "Loser Wins," the tale of a wife who deliberately loses her husband in the jungle. The Strangs' marriage collapses "in an afternoon of astonishing abuse. They had pretended politeness for so long only an afternoon was necessary" (*CF*, 60). Dr. Smith marries the Larut chief in "The Butterfly of the Laruts" and nearly destroys the tribe's traditional life. Even the consul flirts with marriage, meeting an old lover from Africa for a weekend in Singapore in "Diplomatic Relations," but his reticence prevents any renewal of their affair, and she seems perfectly content with her single way of life: "That was her element, diplomatic relations, the continual parting. She was stronger than I had guessed" (*CF*, 198).

Stories reveal dramatic ironies, symmetries, and coincidences,

leading up to surprise endings or making the final denouement a
character study with a scalpel wit. Theroux also delights in creating
the odd character, the stranger who upsets the routine of the insular
and provincial backwater. In Fadila (a crazed local who supposedly
knows the scene) Flint, the Maugham romantic from the embassy,
sees a hospitable connection for the new consul to make use of; the
consul sees only a dirty creature; the upshot reveals a deranged and
abandoned wife: "Her husband took another wife. . . . He went
away and Fadila became an *amok*. Her husband was a devil" (*CF*,
18). People are not as they seem. Margaret Harbottle upsets everyone
and flees disguised as a man. Linda Clem, her affair with the pen-
niless Malayan prince Ilbrahim finished, gets raped by a Malaysian
spirit, an incubus known as "Orang Minyak" in "The Flower of
Malaya." And the consul meets Rao, a former political prisoner,
who remains a totally untrustworthy burnt-out case.

The best stories in the book are those, among others, that suggest
different levels of meaning beyond the mere encounter or character
study. In "Triad" Theroux builds his tale around the number three.
Local children meet in threes, "three Tamils, three Malays, three
Chinese, as if that was the number required for play" (*CF*, 174).
Tony Evans, Rupert Prosser, and the consul meet for drinks at the
Club. The childless Prossers decide to adopt the thin, dirty little
girl Evans discovers in the bushes. "Cleaned up she looked definitely
Chinese. . . . the Prossers . . . were obviously very proud of her"
(*CF*, 177). The trinity is complete: mother, father, daughter, a
family holiness of its own. They name her Nina (one of Columbus's
three ships). "I pictured them in their bungalow on the oil-palm
estate, playing at being a family, as the children in threes played
their games on the Club's grounds" (*CF*, 181).

Gossip at the Club begins to focus on Rupert's relationship with
Nina, who turns out to be sixteen. And one night three men turn
up at the Prossers' house and try to kidnap her. When it happens
again, the consul informs the priest at the mission, Father LeFever.
"They meant to kill her," he explains. "It's the Triad . . . a Chinese
secret society. . . . It is like a religious order. . . . And they
punish impurity their own cruel way. A person is taken and put in
a sack and drowned" (*CF*, 185). The consul guesses that the Triad
has discovered Rupert's affair with her. But Lefever is not thinking
of adultery. The girl's parents have leprosy and live in an isolated
village, from which she had escaped six weeks before. "Even if she's

a carrier," LeFever insists, "it's only infectious if contact has been extensive" (*CF*, 186). The Prossers send the girl back. The consul wonders, "I never found out what had gone on at the Prossers', among those three people; and the Triad was not charged with attempted murder. The only victim was that waif, who was made a leper . . . " (*CF*, 187).

At the leper colony LeFever mentions the visit of a Mr. Leopold: "[H]e and his friend murdered that poor child in Chicago about fifty years ago. It was a celebrated case" (*CF*, 186–87). The holy trinity of parents and child turns unholy, as the tale deepens, and the Triad takes over. A fat Chinese, Pei-Kway, who has first interrogated the girl, wears an interesting tattoo, which the consul thinks links him to the Triad. The unholiest trinity of all turns out to be Leopold, Loeb, and their victim, another child. Suddenly the threesomes at play appear ominous and divisive, parodies of the family structure. Rupert Prosser returns alone to the Club after a long time away. One weekend he has gone to the leprosarium—to see the girl? For a cure? "Evans [the cynical tennis pro and third member of the Club trio—Evans, Prosser, and the consul] became fond of saying, 'I give that marriage six months' " (*CF*, 187).

Other stories stand out. The consul's clever sleuthing involving the "golden handshake" in "The Johore Murders"; the autumnal melancholy of "The Autumn Dog," the title a reference to an awkward Chinese sexual position; the gathering horrors of the ghost stories and gruesome descriptions of corpses, the Horror Tree and the phantom cyclists in "Dengue Fever" and "The Tiger's Suit"; the visit to the rich spoiled sultan and his rich, spoiled daughter in "The Last Colonial." But overall what one remembers is the consul himself, his mordant wit and surprising vulnerability, and the multilayered backwater of Ayer Hitam. The ultimate delight lies in the consul's conviction at the conclusion: "Now I must write my report" (*CF*, 212). The file is complete.

The London Embassy (1983)

Theroux obviously could not let a good character vanish, and so the consul reappears in *The London Embassy*, ready to assess his new post, its social "ins-and-outs," and the various characters he meets in "the center of the civilized world, the best place in Europe, the last habitable city."[15] The same connections between the stories that underlie *The Consul's File* work once again here. The consul has moved on as a political officer to help keep track of influential people, to pursue and cultivate them for basic American interests. It is a perfect setup for a series of separate tales. At the same time the consul retains his previous personality: "It seemed that I had always been a bystander, watching life through a second-story window and expected to talk about the wallpaper. . . . I was always doing something else. My work was my life. I had never been idle" (*LE,* 236). And despite his persistent misgivings—"It was a bachelor's consolation—my job, my office, my hotel room. . . . I hated the implied timidity, the repetition, the lack of surprise in this routine" (*LE,* 39)—yet he maintains, "I am usually happier alone than in company . . . there is a kind of social claustrophobia that afflicts me" (*LE,* 64–65).

In *The London Embassy* we learn more about the consul's background. First and foremost is his name, Spencer Monroe Savage, a secret withheld from us until almost the last line of the book. We also discover that he is an orphan, "bright, solitary, with my trust fund from the insurance money—it was like being privileged, inheriting a title early" (*LE,* 56); his parents were killed in an air crash when he was five.

In the course of this collection Savage becomes involved with three women: Sophie Graveney, "An English Unofficial Rose," who turns out to be more interested in real estate than matrimony; Margaret Duboys, the "heroine" of the story, "Sex and Its Substitutes," who has given her life over to cats of all shapes and sizes and loves them more passionately than her Sunday sex with Savage; and finally Flora Domingo-Duncan, a thirty-two-year-old biographer of Mary Shelley from Bryn Mawr, whose mother is Mexican and who is involved in a group called "Women Opposed to Nuclear Technology." She becomes Savage's wife. In each tale Theroux creates a fine and careful character study of these women, each with her own secrets, each in some way related to embassy functions.

Savage meets Domingo-Duncan at a party given by the American ambassador at Winfield House in "The Winfield Wallpaper," the sixteenth tale in the book. In the consul's eyes Domingo-Duncan far out-dazzles the famous wallpaper in the house, and he breaks off a conversation with Margaret Thatcher—"Even her hair looked hard" (*LE,* 232)—to pursue her. In the following story, "Dancing on the Radio," lust and love coincide, and the consul "grows up"; "All at once, someone else matters to your happiness . . . this solitary life I had been leading was selfish and barren—and turning me into a crank (*LE,* 243) . . . in finding her I had discovered an aspect of my personality that was new to me—a kinder, dependent, appreciative side of me that Flora inspired. If I lost her it would vanish within me and be irretrievable, and I would be the worse for it. . . . It was an elemental desire to establish a society of two" (*LE,* 249–50).

Bad marriages and sexual combat, of course, flourish in *The London Embassy.* Vic Scaduto, the Cultural Affairs Officer at the embassy, is an officious Italo-American on the make. He is raising smug, racist sons in the British mold and harbors a querulous wife who regards herself as a would-be feminist poet. Yuri Kirilov, in "The Honorary Siberian," a self-serving Russian expatriate, offers the consul his sexy, bubble-headed wife Helena in exchange for a visa to the United States. In "Fighting Talk" "This kind of thing happens all the time to married people" (*LE,* 216), Scaduto assures the consul, when someone shoots at Dwight Yorty, a new man in Regional Projects. Through the consul's clever investigations, it becomes clear that Yorty has been set up not by terrorists, as the ambassador and his cronies believe, but by an ex-lover, either Yorty's or his wife's.

In one of the best stories in the collection, "Charlie Hogle's Earring," Everett Horton, the career diplomat and number two man at the embassy, nicknamed "coach," for he believes in the team spirit and is "a hugger, a hand-shaker, a back-slapper" (*LE,* 74)—the kind of macho mover Theroux despises—discovers that Charlie Hogle, a telex operator, is sporting an earring. Regulations, more or less, forbid such things, but Horton overreacts: "That situation was making me sick. . . . I got so mad I actually threw up" (*LE,* 88), causing Savage to wonder about him and his own psychic health. In any case Horton tells Savage to get Hogle to remove it, a process Savage clearly discerns as a way of Horton's testing him to see how tactful his techniques can be and where his ultimate loyalties lie.

Theroux adds depth to the tale by closely observing the inter-relationships between Horton, Savage, and Hogle, at the same time revealing the intricate diplomacies, wasted on an issue so silly, of an embassy staff in practice. Savage takes Hogle to lunch and finds him perfectly ordinary and likable, "an Iowa Lutheran . . . a muscular Christian" (*LE,* 78). And he likes Hogle's earring, "too small to be a pirate's, too simple for a transvestite. I thought it suited him" (*LE,* 79). Hogle wears it because he likes it: "I'm certainly not making any kind of statement. . . . I got the idea from one of the delivery men—an English guy. . . . It looked neat, that's all" (*LE,* 86). But Horton insists, and even though Savage recognizes that "his earring distinguished [Hogle] and made him look like a prince" (*LE,* 82), he's forced to play Horton's hatchetman and informs Hogle the earring goes, or he does.

Since Hogle refuses and Horton insists, Savage tries one more ploy. He sets up an appointment with Hogle in Earl's Court at a pub that is "notoriously male" (*LE,* 84). While Hogle looks at him—"he winced"—Savage praises his earring as "fantastic," as "a real enhancement" (*LE,* 85). The men around them in leather jackets and heavy chains wear earrings as well. Hogle stands up and makes his excuses: "Then he left, and then I removed my earring" (*LE,* 87).

The ploy works; Hogle is scared off; Horton is satisfied. And Savage concludes: "In the following weeks I saw scores of young men Hogle's age wearing earrings. . . . I had made him think there was something dangerous and deviant in this trinket decorating his ear. . . . Hogle would be all right. But after what he had told me, I was not so sure about Horton" (*LE,* 88). In any case Theroux's story, filled with the undercurrents of personalities and professional hierarchies, exposes the inner workings and strategies of the embassy, the American sense of athletic manhood upon which embassy relations are based, the essentially American fears of eccentricity in such relationships, and the political necessity of victimizing the innocent to score points and influence the higher-ups. It is Theroux at his best—compact, concise, "layered" in his interlocking perspectives, with a nice surprise twist at the end.

Racial tensions add to the sexual and social furies of these quiet and understated stories. Erroll Jeeps, a black man at the embassy who sports a harsh, lively humor and loves to tell tales, in "Namesake" tells Savage about the man who came to England to look up his ancestors, one of those typical Americans arrived in "mummified" England to unearth hoped-for aristocratic roots. Baldwick, the man, is white; the man he finally locates turns out to be black, a discordant discovery that parallels the racial distinctions between Jeeps the teller and Savage the listener: "His laughter was humorless.

It was merely a harsh noise, challenging me to look at his black face" (*LE*, 37). Scaduto's insufferable sons refer to "colored boys" as "turdheads"; Savage and Domingo-Duncan make love in "Dancing on the Radio" when the Brixton riots erupt in the streets of London: "It was fierce fighting, sometimes between mobs—blacks and whites fighting—sometimes against the police. . . . It was war out there" (*LE*, 249, 251).

Demented racial prejudice underlies the marvelous story, "The Exile," a superb analysis-exploration of the American expatriate poet, Walter Van Bellamy based loosely on Robert Lowell. Here is a man Savage should cultivate, a man he has looked up to as a writer, having had some idea of writing himself before joining the State Department. In fact, Savage regards Bellamy as "my alter ego . . . at the heart of my quandry was the suspicion that Walter Van Bellamy was a little like me" (*LE*, 100, 101). And what a fascinating personage: looking like a Tory banker yet undergoing spasms of mental unbalance, "eyes as blue as gas flames, a stern bony Pilgrim Father's face" (*LE*, 90), wed three times to wealthy women, so publicly humble he appears arrogant, so intimate in his poetry "it gives nothing away—so private it sounds anonymous" (*LE*, 93). Theroux has a field day limning this man's enigmatic and paradoxical character: socialite, rich, party-goer, guru, conscientious objector, old family name: "To look like a banker and to be known for his nervous breakdown—that was what made him" (*LE*, 91). And his poetry deals with language, culture, and "with a characteristic flourish, he added, 'and schizophrenia' " (*LE*, 93). Above all to Savage and to the reader, he remains a mystery, "and there is nothing in the world harder to know than the private life of a public man" (*LE*, 93).

Through a chance meeting Savage becomes involved in Van Bellamy's private life. The upshot is the consul's visit one night to the Abbey, the private mental hosptial where Bellamy has been put away for awhile. There he discovers the madman revising his poems; his handwriting "indicated disorder and mania and big blue obsession" (*LE*, 104). Bellamy hates Jews. He has entitled one of his poems, "The Jewnighted States." Savage, shocked and sickened, reads one of them: "it was poisonous . . . demented . . . awful, it was wrong . . . babbling about the beauties of Auschwitz" (*LE*, 105, 106). A doctor at the clinic, flashing "a Bellamy smile . . . impatient, patronizing, humorless," explains that "All men are

Nazis, really" (*LE*, 106). In Bellamy's books, published later, Savage finds none of this: "His poems were serene and unmemorable; they never touched these subjects; and afterward, when I couldn't remember them, they frightened me" (*LE*, 107). At the base of the Bellamy mystery: racial hatred with a vengeance, one more glimpse into the darker, unquiet realms at the heart of much of Theroux's fiction, lurking beneath his understated, precise phrases and deliberate ironies.

In Theroux's splendid Gothic tale, revealing again his penchant for Poe, "Tomb With a View," Abdul Wahab Bin Baz, a Muslim lodger, turns out to be a ghoul, nightly robbing the grave of Captain Sir Richard F. Burton: "It was simple revenge. Hadn't Burton, the unbeliever, trampled all over Islam? . . . Burton was no respecter of taboos or traditions—he had plundered the secrets of Islam in his search for adventure" (*LE*, 122). Savage stealthily tracks him down, after exploring the objects in the Muslim's rented room, waits for him one dark night at Burton's Oriental-tent-shaped mausoleum, and buries him alive in the tomb. Later Savage traces a cross in the condensed vapor on the window of the roof of the tomb and shines his flashlight through it down to the young man trapped within: "to the man from Mecca it was strange and unwelcome, and I was sure that it made him more fearful than the darkness he had endured in the tomb all night. It was now safe to remove the padlock: I had announced myself as the avenging Christian" (*LE*, 123).

Theroux spins his Gothic yarn carefully, discovery by discovery, leading up to the shock of discovering a grave robber in action. Before Miss Gowrie, the Muslim's landlady, comes to him asking for help, he has had to deal with a Mrs. Fleamarsh who has had her husand cremated and the ashes delivered into Savage's hands at the embassy. The urn is "the size and shape of a white crock of Gentlemen's Relish. . . . And it put me in the mood for what happened later that day" (*LE*, 108–9), not to mention the reader's mood and expectations as well. Descriptions of the dark and eerie churchyard of St. Mary's, the discovery of the odd trinkets in the Muslim's room, and the shudders throughout add to the deliciously macabre atmosphere and setting of the tale.

Connections are meant to be discovered in *The London Embassy* and elsewhere, such as finding out that it is Walter Van Bellamy who has translated Yuri Kirilov's poetry, "and it was at Bellamy's house in Kent that he had hidden on the day of his defection" (*LE*, 162). Bellamy popped up in "The Odd-Job Man" in *World's End*, as did the consul in that same volume with Charlie and Lois Flint in "Volunteer Speaker." And here in "Fury" Mary Snowfire meets Gretchen, "who told her she was doing graduate work on the European Economic Community, and then smiled and smoothed her chic velvet knickerbockers and said she also worked for an escort agency" (*LE*, 192). Gretchen turns up as Lauren Slaughter in the short novel, *Doctor Slaughter* (1984).

In the first story in *The London Embassy*, "Reception," Savage arrives in London and meets several characters whom he will meet again in the book: "It was a comprehensive list, like 'Cast of Characters' at the opening of a Victorian novel" (*LE*, 14). Theroux carefully sets up, therefore, the structure and the theme of the emblematic and/or eccentric encounters that are to follow. London "had been built to enclose secrets, for the British are like those naked Indians who hide in the Brazilian jungle—not timid, but fanatically private and untrusting. This was a mazy land of privacies. . . . In London, all gardens were behind the houses. They were hidden. 'Plots' was the word" (*LE*, 11, 12). In this the setup for the tales is complete.

One long poem that Walter Van Bellamy read at the poetry night of the London Arts Festival was entitled " 'Londoners,' about Americans in London, starting with Emerson and Hawthorne and ending with himself" (*LE*, 93). Spencer Monroe Savage is also an American in London, an inveterate exile exploring foreign territories, much like Theroux's persona in his travel books. The two share the same keen eye, mordant wit, occasional indignation, and sardonic temper. These provide a perspective that Theroux uses carefully in most of his stories, and one he fully exploits in his longer fictions, where the "savage" eye flourishes best.

Chapter Five

The Early Novels: "A Comedy [and] a Well-Made Ghost Story"

In the early novels Theroux's characteristic techniques and themes are already displayed. The careful observation of detail, the encounters between past and present, the balanced structure and plot of the books, the "deadpan" style with its ironic distance and precise one-liners: all of these techniques emerge in *Waldo* (1967), *Fong and the Indians* (1968), *Murder at Mount Holly* (1969), and *Jungle Lovers* (1971), and in his two early Gothic novels, *Girls at Play* (1969) and *The Black House* (1974). Theroux's continuing themes appear as well: the clash between illusions and realities, between a character's self-image and world he or she operates in, the fragmentation of history with the false unification of myths and wishes, the self confronting an alien landscape. We find the American innocents, the more cosmopolite drifters, the querulous cranks, and the self-enclosed, haunted souls. The lucidity and terror of loneliness confront the alien outpost, rife with hostility, decay, chaos, and the threat of an ultimate entropy. One's identity seems predicated upon one's resistance to that landscape, as if the basic clash between them also results in a mysterious defining of each, the battle for possession of one by the other.

Three Early Novels: "Briefly, a Comedy"

Waldo (1967) reveals the self-conscious artifice of a first novel: the surreal set pieces—the epigraph by Tristan Tzara, the Dadaist, is a good clue to the novel's pacing and sense of itself—the clever chatter, the adolescent angst of Waldo himself, the adolescent rage toward convention and the "normal" that Waldo experiences and expresses, and the quirky and farcical twists and turns of the plot, as our hero proceeds on his spiritual and physical odyssey from the

Booneville School for Delinquent Boys, to Rugg College, the seedy Mandrake Club, and the Bethesda Tesh Zeitgeist Memorial Zoo. James Atlas described *Waldo* as "the rebellious adolescent's diatribe against a foolish, uncomprehending father . . . said by Paul's brothers to be autobiographical. . . . [It is] only the rage of a 26-year-old exacting literary retribution."[1] Theroux, however, attacks and heavily satirizes more than just an uncomprehending father here, as he takes out after college presidents, sensationalist newspapers, psychiatry, and sexual chicanery.

And yet the novel moves and sparkles. It is swift, fast-paced, and reveals the young author's control and sense of language. There are no purple passages of soul-wallowing, which are found in so many first novels; rather this brisk, bright tale already reveals Theroux's talent for irony, observation, and insight. True, the author pauses for "big scenes" about sex and art and love and society. Plot and symbolic utterance do not quite mesh, a sign usually of a young novelist at pains to be both original and profound. But the protagonist's struggle to find an emerging reality, in this case the vocation of writing, parallels Theroux's own amidst a world of callous myths, manipulations, and molestations.

Through his odyssey Waldo slowly discovers the truth of his own imagination, as Theroux was clearly discovering his and jettisoning his Medford background and his own cramped adolescence, exorcising his early rebellion and his imagination's leap. Waldo finally realizes that "It's the stuff you don't know anything about, the stuff that scares you and you're on the verge of hating you've got to write about . . . sweaty stories, nightmares or not" (*W*, 192). After he shoots his aging mistress, he celebrates the knowledge that "he could create and destroy. . . . He had already begun the story, dazzling, uproarious, hilarious, original, vivid" (*W,* 207). And, of course, in cool adolescent self-righteousness he announces that "it didn't have anything to do with love" (*W,* 208). But the commitment to writing comes across honestly and reveals Theroux's self-proclaimed mission to become an artist in his own right to be well earned.

Theroux's experiences in East and Central Africa left him "apologetic and sorrowful, or else very angry [but w]ith *Fong and the Indians* my mood changed: fiction seemed to give me the second chances life denied me. Africa was, briefly, a comedy."[2] Theroux's second novel, a farcical tale set in East Africa, replete with attempted coup d'etats, mistaken identities, curfews, a racial potpourri on the warpath, and canned milk, satirizes the doings of buying and selling, swindles and deals, the marketing of ideologies and goods. Long-suffering Chinese grocer, Sam Fong, is besieged by crafty Indian businessmen, American CIA agents, Chinese Communists, local political thugs, and his own scruples, each trying to command his attention and initiate a final conversion. Each fails in its own way because of miscalculation, circumstance, or farcical discrepancies in the bumptious plot.

Underneath all the comedy and conspiracy, however, lurks a darker reality that Theroux explores at greater length in *Jungle Lovers*. Despite all the turmoil and transgressions "the dull sameness of life in Africa" remains, with its "almost explicit promise that nothing would change" (*FI*, 197). "The disordered slowness . . . in Africa" (*FI*, 198) continues, beneath the farcelike fury between victims and victimizers. When Theroux wrote this slight, spirited novel Africa was, indeed, for him a comedy. But not for long.

His third novel, *Murder in Mount Holly* (1969), is another farcical and satiric jeu d'esprit, a kind of fairy tale which makes fun of old people, superpatriotism, nostalgia, American militarism, prejudice, and, once again, the inadequacy of parents. Charlie Gibbon, Miss Ball, and Mrs. Gneiss, the fat mother of Herbie Gneiss who dies in battle after he has been suddenly drafted, suggest fine Dickensian characters in their cranky, garrulous mannerisms and demeanor. They plot to rob the Mount Holly Trust Company, which they see as "a Communist Front Organisation filled with black pinkoes."[3] The plot pauses to explore the Kant-Brake Toy Factory, a militarist company run by Gen'l Digby, at which both Herbie and Gibbon work—"It was the only place outside of the army itself that made murderous weapons a specialty" (*MMH*, 24)—and then focuses on the elaborate and finally unsuccessful robbery.

In this slight and minor work, along with his first two novels, Theroux lampoons his favorite topics. Age destroys youth; Herbie Gneiss is not as lucky as Waldo. War kills. America's militarism shows up even in its toy shops. Fundamentalist reactionary right-wingers thrive on their own brand of patriotism and prejudice. Theroux caricatures the kind of world he had fled, the America he had abandoned in search of African adventure and involvement. The escalating mayhem in the novel creates a shrill form of satire, but the short book is fun, if one-dimensional and obvious. So much for conservatism, parents, and patriotism in the America of the late 1960s!

Jungle Lovers (1971): "You Have to Import Rags"

In his 1984 preface to his fifth novel, *Jungle Lovers,* Theroux admits to being "struck by its peculiar humor and violence. Some of it is farce and some tragedy. [It is] a novel of futility and failed hopes [which suggest] my mood on leaving Africa" in 1968 after five years in Malawi and Uganda.[4] In his fourth novel, the Gothic *Girls at Play* (1969), which we will examine below, Theroux created a darker, more violent landscape than in his three previous novels, a development that suggests the darkening of his own vision of experience. That darkness emerges once again in *Jungle Lovers* and despite farcical elements produces a richer, more moving fiction than his first three novels.

Jungle Lovers takes place in Malawi, the tiny Central African republic, run by the shrewd, ruthless dictator, Hastings Kanyama Osbong, "a clownish Papa Doc defended by a *Tonton Macoute* of giggling Youth Wingers who, during the day or when it wasn't raining, put up roadblocks and searched for spying Chinese."[5] Malawi is more a tribal than a national state and more a jungle area than a country. According to *Time* magazine, Malawi is suffering from "riot and intrusion, an infant war." Thus "a rumor of death had put Malawi on the American projection of the map, as tulips had done for Holland. That was its claim to statehood: the possibility of its being attacked" (*JL,* 123).

Into this situation comes Calvin Mullet, a divorced insurance agent from Hudson, Massachusetts, intent on selling life insurance policies to the Africans, and Marais, a messianic white revolutionary intent on overthrowing Osbong's corrupt fascist regime and rescuing Malawi for the Africans. The novel chronicles the failure of each to succeed in his appointed task. "I suppose the insurance man and the revolutionary were the two opposing sides of my own personality" (*SS,* 329), Theroux admitted. This essential polarity in the novel—two messianic white men in black Africa, one peddling insurance, the other insurgence—holds the book together nicely, amid the zigs and zags of plot (the more farcical elements), and posits a perilous equilibrium between the possibilities of a secure future and the realities of a brutal and rebellious present.

Both men are also writers. Mullet tries his hand at a novel, *The Uninsured,* under the pseudonym "A. Jigololo," and Marais confides in his notebooks his views about revolution, its tactics, techniques, and prophecies. The one sells insurance to build a future for a fortunate few. The other kills to rescue a fortunate few from a future of slavery and despotism. People and politics battle it out much as individual salvation does political salvation.

In the end Mullet surrenders his ideals of selling insurance, and Marais commits suicide. The white man's role in Africa self-destructs, and life in Africa remains nasty, brutish, and short: in such an "old but narrow culture . . . only death happened to them" (*JL,* 161), the same underlying futility we discovered in *Fong and the Indians,* where "the dull sameness of life in Africa" is alone triumphant.

Calvin Mullet at thirty believes in life insurance and resembles a "striken preacher" (*JL,* 8). He fears the "jungle dark" (*JL,* 109) but wants to offer comfort, to eradicate insecurities and despair through a more secure future. He genuinely likes Africans, but when his Malawian friend Ogilvie is murdered by Marais's revolutionaries, he realizes that in terms of selling insurance, "there was no future in it; Africans needed it like a hole in the head" (*JL,* 157). He feels he has been deluded: "[I]t was cruel to make them think that they could be saved by insurance. . . . Nothing changed, not even a death in the family altered them, insurance never could" (*JL,* 161). Thus "it was a relief to be rid of that impulse to preach, that yen to save lives" (*JL,* 158). Yet his sense of drift reveals his lost cause, and only his marriage to Mira, Ogilvie's sister, and the birth of his son renew his interest in doing something, if only escape seems inevitable.

On the other hand stands Marais, at twenty-seven "the Lone Ranger" (*JL,* 151), the terrorist as idealist, as consummate liberator. He admires Che Guevara and like him writes about revolution and rebellion in his *Principles of Revolt.* He writes lyrically of revolutionary principles, but as the real revolt gets underway, his rhetoric changes: "It was a beginner's impractical rhetoric. . . . Poetry was a clever reply, an illness of the ear, a lying substitute for a coarse truth. The subject was obscured by the poet's self-importance . . . symbols were bubbles, falsifying, making brutality into a lyric" (*JL,* 175). Slowly as the rebellion gains momentum and his troops take the town of Lilongwe, his textbook becomes a diary, a brutal revelation of events and his own diminishing place in them.

Finally Marais's black soldiers mutiny and place him under house arrest. He loses his military control, realizing the tenuous place of a white man in a black man's revolt, seeing himself accepted and despised at the same time, finding himself imprisoned in his own solitary role. He laments his fate: "They don't trust me . . . I'm alone. . . . I am an enemy, a witch. . . . It used to be *We, Us;* now it's *Them* and *They*" (*JL,* 244). He realizes that Osbong's failure to recognize his rebellion and act against it has efficiently sabotaged it, and that tribal connections and hatreds mean more than political revolution in such a place. Haunted and naked, he knows his end is at hand and that his mission is doomed, thus echoing one of the novel's epigraphs from Arthur Rimbaud, "J'ai seul la clef de cette parade sauvage" (I have the only key to this savage parade). He plunges into a fire to destroy his notebooks—and himself.

Mullet's manuscript reveals black rage against exploiters of all kinds, and both Marais and Mullet acknowledge that each has exploited the African in his own way. "A. Jigololo" urges blacks to rise up. Mullet chooses lines from poet Wallace Stevens for his epigraph: "Death, only, sits upon the serpent throne: / Death, the herdsman of elephants . . . and Africa, basking in antiquest sun, / Contains for its children not a gill of sweet" (*JL,* 102–3). Mullet gives up on his manuscript; even rage becomes no longer valid for him, as he drifts out of the insurance game. And yet the irony occurs when his assistant Mwase, hired by the state when Mullet's insurance office is nationalized, steals the manuscript, and it becomes a pamphlet in the revolution, "his stolen book being passed around and crazing the Africans" (*JL,* 291). Words can kill, and Mullet's and Marais's fascination with them reveals both characters' messianic fervor and their failure to succeed in their stated missions.

Theroux strengthens the polarity of his two major characters by structuring his novel in a similar manner. He consistently skips back and forth from chapter to chapter between Mullet and Marais, juxtaposing their private battles and enduring failures. The balanced structure of the novel—a key Therouxvian technique—holds it together, although at times it might appear to be too tidy, too neatly arranged, once the connections are discovered. It calls attention to itself in a way that may be detrimental to the novel's power and scope, but it foreshadows Theroux's superb and subtle use of such structural balancing acts in more accomplished novels such as *The Black House* and *The Mosquito Coast*.

Doublings multiply within the text and add a resonance and depth it would otherwise lack. Mira and Mullet are described as "jungle lovers" (*JL*, 184), although Mullet and Marais could be described in similar terms. As Theroux suggests in commenting on Mira and Mullet, "Lovers might be opposites, but duration always turned them into twins" (*JL*, 167). Racial animosities explode, as black battles white. The blacks at first look to white men for leadership, at the same time as they despise them. To lead and to be imprisoned in the role of leadership are similar fates.

Throughout *Jungle Lovers* Theroux insistently undercuts the myth of empire. Major Beaglehole, an unregenerate British colonialist who wishes the days of empire were back, is constantly ridiculed and brought up short by the events and other characters around him. His is a voice crying in an African wilderness, to which no one will listen. The Moth's Club on the Chikwawa Road, where unregenerate Britishers hang out, suggests the provincially isolated club in Ayer Hitam with its creaking British codes reduced to anecdote and reminiscence. And Osbong's dictatorship is no better, as brutal and as calculated as it is. Both the past and present are grim, and the future seems to bode only ill.

The persistent doubling in the novel ultimately suggests the cyclical and futile patterns that Theroux establishes there: from colonialism to independence to dictatorship to a constant series of revolts and revolutions to dictatorship once again. Does it really make any difference if Osbong or Brother Jaja, the black leader of the opposition, is in charge? Both men hate, kill, and act solely out of self-interest and revenge. Tribal patterns outweigh any possible national or political union that can make Theroux's Malawi a viable national entity.

Blacks and whites tangle, regroup, and tangle again with no apparent progress. The cycle may suggest farce, but the cost in human life produces brutal and tragic realities. All tumbles into the abyss of such recognitions: "White is *all* colors. But black—it is not a color at all" (*JL*, 265). That all-color, no-color antithesis suggests Herman Melville's terrified and terrifying universe of an ultimate blind atheism that leads nowhere but to dissolution and despair.

Beneath Theroux's carefully crafted structure and polarized char-acters lies this knowledge, eased somewhat by the balance of his prose and careful doublings, but finally brutally clear. "We are hopeless," says Mwase. "Hobbies—have you read Thomas Hobbies [*sic*]? He was right, life in Africa is nasty, British and short. . . . This country is a jail and Osbong is the in-charge" (*JL*, 265). All are prisoners of "a patch of jungle in central Africa . . . a political accident . . . it was bankrupt. Its one factory, Chiperoni Blankets Ltd., had to import rags from Italy to make the blankets. Calvin had heard it with astonishment: *You have to import rags?*" (*JL,* 122).

Girls at Play (1969): "The Green Riotous Disorder"

The polarities, the futility, and the disintegration of *Jungle Lovers* constitute a Gothic nightmare in Theroux's fourth novel, *Girls at Play*. The Marais and Mullet of the fifth novel appear in the fourth as self-destructive doubles in a world fraught with murderous thoughts, rape, suicide, psychic collapse, and actual murder. It is a Poesque world, where order becomes obsessive and by its very obsessive nature incurs its own destruction, a nightmare realm where opposites repel each other but are dependent upon each other for their identity. Vampirish spirits attack and ravage one another; mirror images pursue mirror images of one another. The whole claustrophobic catastrophe resembles a place of entrapment and iso-lation that can only collapse under its own weight.

The battlelines are drawn between Miss Poole, the headmistress of a girls' school in East Africa, and the new teacher, Heather Monkhouse. Poole, born in East Africa, fled in 1952, when her father's farm was attacked, and spent a solitary eight-year exile in England before returning. Upon her return she can see only a country violated by a black takeover—"It was being trampled. . . . The whole place was undeniably fouled"[6]—and she yearns for the lost racist order her father's generation had so successfully maintained. Only forty, she looks sixty and suffers from paranoid fears of intru-sion, attack, and failure: "Miss Poole's was a face illustrating extreme fatigue, paranoia, bush fever, and other symptoms of dry anxiety" (*GAP*, 167). Her sense of order borders on obsession, fraught with a "queer consistency" in all things, and she remains a friendless, hypochondriacal spinster-martinet at her school, living only with

her foul-smelling cats. It is little wonder that she views Heather
Monkhouse as a threat, a witch, a killer: "Miss Poole saw her as a
demon-figure, corrupt, lustful, lower-class. . . . Heather had
brought the disorder, cruelty and death which Miss Poole associated
with all the intruders that had ever plagued Africa" (GAP, 120,
121).

Heather Monkhouse is no saint. Formerly a salesgirl in the Stork
Shoppe in Croydon, she is thirty-six but thinks of herself as girlish.
She enjoys her promiscuity, her "capacity for affairs" that usually
end in disaster. She yearns to be a high-class call girl and has come
to Nairobi to be reborn: "Unlike London, it was filled with attractive
people; no one was poor. There were bachelors everywhere . . .
long gay parties. . . . She had become young, upper-middle-class,
desirable. . . . [H]er house in one of Nairobi's lovely suburbs was
surrounded by flowers; there were servants" (GAP, 23). Hers is the
colonialist fairy tale come true. "Oh, but I'm rather like that English
girl in the Maugham story," she tells a passenger aboard ship on
her way to East Africa. "Very lucky, you know. I'll meet a tea
planter and he'll see me through" (GAP, 16). Loveless, she will
triumph in such a racist paradise, a paradise, of course, for whites
only, for British whites.

Heather suffers from what Theroux had diagnosed as seeking the
white "life-style" in a black country. His list of four reasons for
going to Africa, according to this diagnosis, parallels Heather's own:
"An active curiosity in things strange; a vague premonition that
Africa rewards her visitors; a wish to be special; and an unconscious
desire to stop thinking and let the body take over."[7] Heather Monkhouse embodies those characteristics beautifully in her grotesquely
girlish manner. And racism, as Theroux has pointed out, "the passive assertion . . . of color," underlies it all: "All of this information
is slanted toward white superiority, the African as animal . . . the
result is a definite feeling of racial superiority" (SS, 34). The upshot
comes inevitably: "The realization that he is white in a black country, and respected for it, is the turning point in the expatriate's
career. . . . The standard of expatriate living is always very
high. . . . There is the death of the mind . . . to be white is to
be right; being British is an added bonus . . . fascism is easy . . .
Within the slowly decaying condition of mind that is realised after
years of sun and crowds, disorder and idleness, is a definite racial
bias" (SS, 35, 36, 38). Heather remains bitchy and cynical, "the

noisy one that wears all the makeup on her face," (*GAP*, 193) according to Fitch, the owner and operator of the local pub.

It is precisely that "definite racial bias" that locks Poole and Monkhouse in mortal combat, in addition to their psychological characteristics and expectations: the lustful, promiscuous creature in contrast to the spinsterish, paranoid headmistress. At one point Poole hollers at Heather: "My Africans are better than your Africans!" (*GAP*, 78) as if the spoils were to be divided unequally.

Heather is transferred from a large girls' school in Nairobi to Miss Poole's smaller school out in the bush. We learn later that she had had an affair in the city, became pregnant, was operated on for a uterine cyst, was arrested for disturbing the peace, and was consequently transferred. The moment she arrives, her dog attacks one of Miss Poole's cats, thus beginning a long and far-ranging feud between the two women. The battle escalates, until Miss Poole's black servant Julius attacks Heather's Jacko. Both servants eventually flee, but "the games had turned from a ritual of hateful play to hate itself; the symbolic gesture of dislike was now explicitly violent" (*GAP*, 101).

Meanwhile another teacher, Bettyjean (B. J.) Lebow, an outgoing, naive American from the Peace Corps, has met Wangi, a black man and the cousin of the District Education Officer, Wilbur, who has just been transferred from Nairobi. She suggests a typical American with her sinless face, her generosity of spirit, and her genuine innocence in and ignorance of the world at large. She views the British as contemptible poseurs playing out their old, cynical roles. Wangi remains darkly silent and continues to stare at her, looking like "a crouching Congolese figurine, hard, glossy, black, representing something" (*GAP*, 61). He admits to having taken part in the Mau-Mau rebellion against the British and having killed some of them. But B.J. has always wanted to date a "Host Country National." With Wangi she goes to visit his village and is shocked, since it looks like a "tropical slum." As they return, B.J. suggests that Wangi ask his cousin Wilbur to date Heather.

At the Horse and Hunter, the local pub, Wilbur and Heather, much against her will, and B.J. and Wangi drink together. Wilbur knows about Heather's history in Nairobi, since he had been the assistant District Education Officer there—"I remember your case"—so she pretends to seduce him in order to keep him quiet. Back at Heather's house, Wilbur attempts to blackmail her for sex but slips and knocks himself out. The next morning Miss Poole summons Heather to her office: "You want to be me!" (*GAP*, 169) she declares. Heather announces her resignation, just as Pamela Male, another teacher at school, timid and colorless but loyal, informs her that B.J. has locked herself in her room and will not come out. In fact Wangi has raped B.J. the night before, and a disoriented, horrified B.J. wanders off to drown herself.

The novel rushes to its horrifying climax. Miss Male goes to the police to report that B.J. is missing. Miss Poole talks with Wilbur, hoping that he will help her to force Heather to leave, not knowing of the previous night's complications. At this point Fitch's sidekicks find B.J.'s body, Miss Male identifies it and whimpers sadly, "I want to go home." The police escort a distraught Miss Poole from the school, and Wilbur installs Heather as headmistress in an effort to cover his own tracks. In talking to Miss Male, Heather confesses about her affair in Nairobi, about her promiscuity in general, and says that she will reveal to the police Wilbur's bribe of making her headmistress. Relieved, she falls asleep. But Rose, Miss Poole's servant, an albino who must wear dark glasses to cover her scorched eyes, sneaks into Heather's room with Miss Poole's carving knife and hacks her to pieces. We last see Rose standing on the main lawn of the school, "a white mottled dwarf, one arm across her stricken eyes against the agony of the afternoon sun" (*GAP,* 210).

Throughout the novel Theroux has buttressed his vision of psychic warfare and collapse by emphasizing the precarious balance between order and chaos everywhere. In the opening paragraph the hockey field confronts the surrounding jungle: "The flame trees enclosed the hockey field in a high leafy wall of bulging green. . . . On all sides of the field were green juicy barriers; an African cage, comfortable and temporary. . . . The order seemed both remote and unreasonable." That "bulging green" seems to threaten the ordered field; a wary state of equilibrium reveals within it "swamp dwellers tuning up for the night," the green riotous disorder of African jungle and alien landscape. And the image of the temporary cage suggests a repressive environment, a place that cannot last: "If the fat black girls had not been there and playing, the order of this playing field in the highlands of East Africa would terrify" (*GAP*, 1).

Such order produces and invites its own antidote. As in Carson McCullers's nightmarish *Reflections in a Golden Eye,* the imposed order of Miss Poole's girls' school suggests McCullers's army post in peacetime, a place where sexual repressions flower and fester. Heather Monkhouse becomes the sexually charged, unstable intruder into Miss Poole's closed, claustrophobic world, just as Private Williams in McCullers's novel intruded upon the unstable sexual relationships of the army post and brought them to a boil. In both books an obsession with order necessarily yields to and conjures up its counterpart in disorder and violence. An older masculine violence, associated with Wangi and Wilbur, disrupts the fragile female repressions and destroys them all.

Theroux increases the nightmarish battlelines by his consistent use of opposites. Miss Poole and Heather are only the most obvious pair. We find the image patterns of order and disorder, the cultural clashes between black and white, Africa and England, America and England, men and women, the school and the jungle, culminating in such ultimate confrontations as that between flesh and spirit— "The outraged mind and undecided body were two separate things" (*GAP,* 179)—between the lush countryside and death: "Africa was green, even lush, but lushness made death possible. B.J. had died in a clutter of flowers; there were petals on her dead face" (*GAP,* 197).

In the structure of the novel and in his style Theroux parallels the constricted doubleness and battling opposites of his plot and vision. Alternate chapters reinforce that vision. Chapters 2 and 4, for instance, focus on Miss Poole; chapters 3 and 5, on Heather. In chapter 6 the dog attacks the cat. If chapter 7 is B.J.'s chapter, chapter 8 must be Wangi's. In chapter 11 we get games; in chapter 12, silence. Myths of Africa are explored in the successive chapters entitled "Silence," "Orders," and "A Banana Peel." At the same time Theroux's style stalks his characters. It reminds the reader of the progress of B.J.'s recurring nightmare about her rape, "proceeding with horrifying and deliberate efficiency, increasing in clarity" (*GAP,* 177). Almost mercilessly Theroux reveals his characters' illusions about themselves, holding them up for the reader to scrutinize, never forgetting that what look like illusions to us, to the characters remain their primary explanation of themselves, their hopes, and their fears.

The title itself, *Girls at Play,* reveals final ironies. What begins as a kind of vicious, bitchy feud dissolves into rape and murder. On the hockey field one may hear "the fuguing screech of the girls at play," but one is also aware of "the swamp and the stream . . . where many demon workers hammered and sawed near dusk but . . . produced nothing more than a penetrating swamp smell" (*GAP*, 44). To Heather "there's nothing worse than a bunch of women together. . . . We're all so damned bloodthirsty . . . we're like some breed of ghastly bird, always pecking and clawing" (*GAP*, 73–74). Her summary is succinct: "We're all bitches, aren't we?" (*GAP*, 103), perhaps revealing once again that misogynist undercurrent in most of Theroux's fiction. Ultimately these white women, no matter their ideologies and longings, remain "exiles . . . unmarried among bananas . . . they had asked for it" (*GAP*, 206). And the whole African adventure had produced "only the endless staring of Wangi, the bitchery of Heather and Miss Poole and the noisy aimlessness of the girls at play" (*GAP*, 111).

Africa itself takes on many guises, depending upon one's individual perception of it. For Rose, Africa seems "the kind balance, the calm order, that love caused. . . . Africa breathed peace, not a skull-shape on the map, but the head of God, Christ brooding over the rest of the threatening world" (*GAP*, 125–26). Heather imagines Africa at first as "a huge black carcass, inert in the ocean, with evil at its center" (*GAP*, 18) and thinks of her journey into the bush, the highlands of East Africa, as "a thousand years back in time, now among people who uttered magic, dug with small pointed sticks, and with shards of glass circumcised little girls spread on mats" (*GAP*, 38). Miss Poole's Africa remains the order imposed by and on her father's farm, a notion undercut by Wangi's and Wilbur's violent anti-British resentment of such order. And Fitch, the pub owner, "had read and enjoyed Graham Greene, and there was a time when he had consciously modeled his drinking and generally squalid appearance on the unhappy expatriates in the Greene books. . . . After several years of working at it, the character *was* Fitch; it was no longer a pose" (*GAP*, 144).

Of all these personal visions of Africa, however, Theroux pays the most attention to B.J.'s disillusioned view of it, intimated in the novel's epigraph taken from André Gide's *Travels in the Congo:* "I must confess I am a little disappointed with the forest. I hope to find better elsewhere. The trees are not very high; I expected more shade, more mystery and strangeness. . . ." B.J. feels cheated

and rehearses a long soliloquy filled with African myths and stereotypes she had been raised on, everything from drums and festivals
to "the sun setting on the Empire . . . Mistah Kurtz . . . Papa
Hemingway bushwhacking through lion country . . . [and] voo-
doo" (*GAP,* 109, 110). Now all of this "was a lot of baloney. It
existed only in movies, books and people's crazy imaginations"
(*GAP,* 110). Explorers had faith in and perpetuated such myths.
But the real Africa remains "only disorganized, slow and dull"
(*GAP,* 111), boring, silent, and empty: "In the silence was all of
Africa's cruel ambiguity, what people took for mystery; it was not
mystery. . . . It was a huge bluff" (*GAP,* 131). Even Wangi,
whom she wildly overestimates to her peril, seems only simple and
dull. And the real Africa turns out to be "a tropical slum. . . .
In this ripe pile of garbage was the image. Not drums, dancers or
exotic birds, but a special laughable silence. . . . *Africa is a banana
peel*" (*GAP,* 138).

   Girls at Play, James Atlas has suggested, "is ostensibly about the
internecine psychological warfare waged by two spinsterish schoolteachers in the East African bush, but its real subject is the futility
of African politics and the disintegration of tribal life."[8] While
Atlas's remarks are observant, they miss the Gothic underpinnings
of Theroux's vision. In *Girls at Play* Theroux gave full reign to his
Poesque talents, that nightmarish vision which so far has reached
its fullest embodiment in his seventh novel, *The Black House.* That
Gothic vision is always there in his later fiction—in the urban
warfare of *The Family Arsenal,* in the incestuous background of
Maude Coffin Pratt's photographic art in *Picture Palace,* and in the
mad Honduran schemes of Allie Fox in *The Mosquito Coast*—but
Theroux first developed it in *Girls at Play.*

   The power of the novel resides not in its horrors but in its carefully
crafted atmosphere, the nightmarish realm of psychic imprisonment
and vampirish battles of will, that sense of a pervasive warfare
between possession and being possessed, akin to the kind of battles
in Henry James's *The Turn of the Screw.* The obvious patterning and
doubling may indicate a young author's still feeling his way toward
the sweep and authentic power of *The Mosquito Coast,* but the Gothic
craft is clearly there. "My real weakness is for a well-made ghost
story,"[9] Theroux once wrote. *Girls at Play* reveals his early and
decisive ambitions in that area.

The Black House (1974): "The Menace Was the Shadow"

Theroux's seventh novel abandons Africa, though not entirely, for Dorset, England, and conjures up a Gothic tale of sexual possession, which includes elements of witchcraft, a haunted dark house, and the isolation of a mind trapped in its own fears and anxieties. Alfred Munday's consciousness broods over the whole of the novel, as central to it as the querulous, cranky perspectives yet to come of Maude Coffin Pratt in *Picture Palace* and Allie Fox in *The Mosquito Coast*. At the same time comparisons and contrasts between English and African villages—Munday has spent ten years with the Bwamba tribe in Uganda compiling his anthropologist's notes—that at first appear decidedly different from one another, collapse in upon each other, leaving only a consciousness of mutual isolation and witchcraft as their legacy. As in *Girls at Play,* antitheses tumble into a darker synthesis, as would-be sorcery overwhelms the obstinate and arrogant Munday and leaves him a victim of his own worst fears and desires. A legacy of loneliness ultimately consumes him, the worst Therouxvian fate.

After ten years in Africa, Alfred and his wife Emma decide to retire in Dorset, ostensibly because of Alfred's heart condition. They move into the locally infamous "Black House" in the village of Four Ashes where Alfred intends to write a book on his African experiences. The local vicar suggests that Munday give a lecture at the church hall. With some sadistic delight, he discusses circumcision ceremonies and passes several weapons among the aged listeners. Meanwhile, Emma has seen a mysterious woman gazing out the window of their upstairs bedroom, and Munday, on a walk across the countryside, has discovered two dead dogs—" [T]hey had been killed, and Munday thought flayed"[10]—at a local's (Hosmer's) cottage.

At the Awdrys' New Year's Eve party in Four Ashes, Caroline Summers makes her appearance and entrances Munday. Emma tells him that Caroline was the woman she saw in the upstairs window, feels suddenly unwell, and Munday drives her home. He then returns to the party to see Caroline again, and the two of them drive to the Black House to make love voraciously near the fireplace there. Munday becomes possessed by his lust for Caroline, so much so that he ignores a former African friend, Silvano, who comes to the village to visit him. On a trip to Hosmer's cottage, sent there by Emma to get some apples, he meets Caroline again, and they resume their passionate sex. He meets Caroline a third time in a churchyard, and she tells him that she has used Emma to contact him: "I can only reach you through her" (*BH*, 183). He also learns later that Emma is the one with the heart condition, not him.

The climax occurs when Emma invites Caroline to dinner. Munday learns that the dead dogs belonged to her, and that probably Hosmer killed them in some act of revenge against her, the "liberated" widow. Emma, after asking Caroline to spend the night, goes off to bed leaving the illicit lovers one more opportunity to have sex. Caroline exclaims that the Black House had once belonged to her, and that they both need Emma: "You don't know what they'd do if it got around that Emma left. They've already stolen my dogs. . . . If you want me you must keep her" (*BH*, 241). Munday sleeps, awakes to find Emma still sound asleep and Caroline gone, and recognizes that "the Black House matched Africa, and it was . . . falling in upon itself, crushed by its own weight and size" (*BH*, 245).

He decides to leave Four Ashes with Emma, as if his sexual obsession has subsided at last—he has had sex with Caroline three times, the same number as with his mistress, Claudia Mills, in Africa, whom he has visited in London—and is puzzled that Emma is still sound asleep: "He sat in the empty room, studying the dead fire, and waited for Emma to wake" (*BH*, 245). Theroux implies that Emma, in fact, has died during the night, and Munday has lost both his faithful if downtrodden wife and his sensual if forever elusive mistress. The Black House has worked its vengeance, and he sits in total isolation, observing only the dead ashes of his hopes, his passions, and his self-identity.

Throughout the novel Alfred Munday remains haunted by elusive, unsettling forces. His public personality remains aloof, disdainful, and arrogant, for he acts rudely toward the locals and bullies Emma in his narcissistic, self-centered manner, the kind Caroline describes in general terms as "the ugly kind, posturing, preening yourself before other people, making them acknowledge you" (*BH*, 239). But in his own mind "it was as if someone . . . was hunting him . . . a presence that the apparent emptiness warned him of" (*BH*,

23). He feels restless, anxious, aimless, and displaced. When Emma tells him of the woman at the window, he recognizes, "she had seen what he loathed and dreaded, she had named his fear" (BH, 56).

The Black House comes to represent Munday's fears, suggesting as it does a closed environment like his own consciousness, a haunted place of strange noises and mysterious intruders. In a dream Munday conjures up "a tall house on a black landscape . . . like his own, with a black slate roof, but (and this woke him) it had no doors or windows" (BH, 53). And when he looks back at it out on a walk with Emma, "it seemed a place blighted by age, stained dark like the nightmare house with no windows or doors he had seen in his dream at this exact angle" (BH, 59). The house coincides with his "rediscovery of old fears, aimlessness he hadn't bargained for, and a feeling of age and loss he mocked in a way that seemed to make his mockery an expression of greater fear" (BH, 49). And "the irregular contours of the broken dripping stone" feel to him, "as if he were facing his own guilt" (BH, 152).

Munday's recognition of his fears culminates in his explanations of the isolation of African villages and of reality in his talk in the church hall. In an African village people are cut off from the rest of the world; "they withdraw to a shadowy interior world. This inspires certain fears—irrational fear, you might say, is a penalty of that isolation . . . everything else is mysteriously threatening" (BH, 70, 71). It is as though he were talking about his own obstinate but precarious isolation. And his ideas about reality? "It is a guess, a wish, a clutch of fears, an opinion offered without any hope or proof . . . a series of arrogant notions inspired by the sharpest fear" (BH, 72).

He goes on, speaking directly to Emma in the audience: "We accept what reality is bearable and try to ignore the rest, because we know it would kill us to see it all. . . . It would be interesting to see how we invent one another" (BH, 72). Much later he recognizes that in his observations of the Bwamba, in "describing their lives, giving new definition to their culture, promoting their uniqueness, he was inventing them" (BH, 216). In any case the fears remain, and his main fear "was of being hunted down, thrown out of the Black House by a gulping phantom" (BH, 88).

The "gulping phantom" turns out to be Caroline Summers, but she does not throw him out of the Black House; after their first overheated sexual encounter there, she restores him to it: "The Black

House was finally his, and it was Caroline's doing: she knew the house, she had directed him here. . . . It was deliberate" (*BH*, 161). What Munday comes to recognize is that his fears have culminated in his illicit sexual desires for Caroline, that his anxious aimlessness is once more in search of a passionate affair outside the bland conventions of his marriage to Emma. In his isolated, self-serving justifications for his actions, he convinces himself that in terms of Emma, "what she feared he desired . . . her fear had obsessed her in the same way as his desire. But she had deprived him of his pleasure . . . it was not fear at all" (*BH*, 141).

In Africa Munday "had entered the culture and assisted in practices whose value he saw only as an active participant; witchcraft and sorcery had almost brought him to belief in those early years because he had been more than a witness" (*BH*, 6). He feared not that he was "incapable of understanding the witch-ridden mind in the village paralyzed by myth, but of understanding it too well" (*BH*, 185). Caroline embodies these bewitching qualities, and Munday realizes what has happened: "now the phantom was flesh; he was possessed; he was complete, and Emma was a stranger to him" (*BH*, 159).

Slowly Munday's observations of Africa and England, at first completely separate, begin to reflect one another, achieve a kind of similarity and oneness that suggest the force of his surrender to Caroline's bewitching powers. At the very beginning of the novel, when he and Emma are staying in the guest wing of the Yew Tree, the local pub, he wonders, "Have I carried Africa here?" (*BH*, 10), fearful that he cannot escape African dark nights, the jungle, and the seclusion. During his church talk he begins to perceive the similarities between the isolation and tribal rites of both African and English villages: "The isolation they have in common is the very thing that isolates them from each other" (*BH*, 71). And finally he decides that "he had returned to find Africa in England, not the whole of Africa, but a handful of its oldest follies. In some respects the two places were identical in mood, in the size of their customs" (*BH*, 208). In one respect they are all one: the isolation, Munday's fears and desires, Caroline's possession of him, the elusive suggestions of witchcraft and necromancy. "All I needed to know about isolation and perhaps even tribalism [is] right here in Four Ashes," Munday tells Caroline, "and witchcraft . . . of a sort. Anyway that love of Africa . . . is like sexual voyeurism" (*BH*, 226).

It is Emma, Munday concludes, whom the Black House has victimized, not realizing to the end how much it represents his own doomed narcissistic self-encapsulation: "it was a house so veiled you imagined a victim in one of its darkened rooms. He had thought it was himself; for a while—but without knowing her name—he believed it was Caroline; now he knew it was Emma" (*BH*, 224).

Emma hated Africa and Alfred's superiority toward the Bwamba. She meets his blustering arrogance with her own primness and acquired calmness, sustaining and encouraging him. Munday relies on her, takes her for granted, ignores her pleas for love, and talks only of himself, of the book he will never write, of his own pet peeves and querulous despairs. She dreams of sex with him and tries to initiate it herself; he ignores her. At last he learns it is *her* heart trouble that has driven them from Uganda, not his. And she upbraids him: "You never help me!" (*BH*, 166).

It is Caroline who recognizes the necessity of Munday's staying with Emma, not merely to avert village rumors and revenge but for Caroline's necromantic messages: "I can only reach you through her." The ritualistic formalities of Munday's affair with Caroline are quickly established: "Munday waited for Caroline to contact him through Emma—it had become a ritual for him. . . . He looked to Emma for Caroline's signal" (*BH*, 202). It is Emma who sends him to Hosmer's for the apples and to the churchyard and who finally invites Caroline to dinner and to spend the night. In fact, Munday realizes that "the desire he felt for Emma became a yearning for Caroline—it was intense, bearing on one, then the other, a sexual blessing Emma inspired that he would bestow on Caroline . . . the flutter in his blood" (*BH*, 234). He cannot do without either one.

After their third sexual revel and after falling asleep, Munday wakens, hoping that Emma will forgive him, as if Caroline has restored him to her, and the enchantment with his mysterious incubus is over: "He had been haunted, and though Emma had slept through it all . . . she had always been with him" (*BH*, 245). After Claudia in Africa, there was Emma. After Caroline in Dorset, he hopes Emma will still be there. But Emma has not awakened by the novel's end, and the Black House's "falling in upon itself, crushed by its own weight and size," suggests Munday's own collapse like some black hole in a solitary universe, utterly alone and bereft. The fire is not the only thing that lies dead in the Black House.

Waldo, Sam Fong, Calvin Mullet, and Marais, Miss Poole, Heather Monkhouse, and Bettyjean LeBow have all been outsiders, whether in their native land or in Africa. Alfred Munday is the ultimate outsider, both in his native land and in Africa. As Awdry suggests, "Every outsider is suspect here. But if I may say so, the outsider who antagonizes locals is a liability to the rest of us. One is expected to come to terms with the village. This hasn't happened in your case" (*BH*, 217). Munday remains an outsider, unable and unwilling to participate fully in any society or culture, his own or others', and the result or the reason lies in his own prideful isolation, whether visible in public arrogance or invisible in his own private fears. He is the prototype of the Therouxian hero, the isolated observer thrown back on his own inner resources that prove self-deluding, harden into shrill dogmatic beliefs, and/or determine his own demise.

Around and within this character all of Theroux's themes and techniques coalesce: the eye for detail, the undercutting of others' myths and self-delusions (more often than not excluding one's own), the recognition of a separate self in an alien landscape (whether at home or abroad), which both threatens and helps to define one's own identity. And in the novels themselves Theroux doubles and redoubles such perceptions, intensifying them, producing Gothic fears and/or constitutive opposites that reinforce his initial vision. The careful balancing may blunt the darker vision in these earlier novels, but in the elusive and indeterminate ending of *The Black House,* such structural balancing opens out into darker uncertainties, the fears, guilts, and solitude epitomized in the Black House itself. In that small dark Dorset village Theroux discovered one of his best novels, the culmination of his novelistic apprenticeship—with the exception of *Saint Jack* (1973), which will be discussed in the next chapter—and the more nightmarish revelations of the lucidity of his loneliness.

Chapter Six

The Later Novels: "The Sheer Power of Self-Creation"

Theroux once admitted, "There is a way in which all the books are in a chain. In *Saint Jack* the character Leigh speaks of wanting to retire to the country, and in my next novel, *The Black House,* a man actually does that, while at the end of *The Black House,* 'he craved a simpler world,' at which point I went on the Great Railway Bazaar—simple world—and wrote about a Vietnam dropout . . . and the upshot was *The Family Arsenal,* which ends with a craving for Guatemala, which occurred in *The Old Patagonian Express;* and in that book in two places I indicated that I was planning *The Mosquito Coast.* . . . I have I think been ploughing the same furrow."[1]

In the later novels Theroux widens that furrow and extends his reach. The four major characters in the four novels—Jack Fiori in *Saint Jack* (1973), Valentine Hood in *The Family Arsenal* (1976), Maude Coffin Pratt in *Picture Palace* (1978), and Allie Fox in *The Mosquito Coast* (1982)—carry the burden of a wider vision than any of Theroux's earlier characters. In Jack Fiori we see the promise of the American spirit and consciousness. In Allie Fox we discover its darker, destructive side. Maude Coffin Pratt wrestles with the ineradicable paradoxes between life and art, photographic surfaces and real people, memories and revelations. Valentine Hood struggles with the intricacies of revenge, urban terrorism, the burden of contemporary violence, and the shadows of peculiarly American guilts. In each case the main character, knowingly or not, translates his or her own moral vision into a larger myth, and Theroux laces his tales with allegorical and symbolic elements to support and extend the ramifications of that myth.

Saint Jack (1973): "Tangible Grace"

Jack Fiori, fifty-three, born in 1918 in the North End of Boston, pimps and scrimps in Singapore, "a sort of pornocrat"[2] who yearns for wealth, "success, comfort, renown, the gift that could be handled, tangible grace" (*SJ*, 79). He decides to write a book, in which the main character is named Jack Flowers who will go on "to discover the simplicity of love and the surprise of wealth." Fiction, he believes (as does Theroux), will "give me the second chances life denied me" (*SJ*, 108), but life becomes too complex for him to stick to his writing regimen. He continues to wear his flowered, open-necked shirt as his trademark, along with his white shoes, and acts the clown whenever possible: "I turned my worst pains into jokes to make myself small and to obscure my sick aches; it was my fear of being known well and pitied—my humour was motivated by humility" (*SJ*, 135). He becomes an "unassertive rascal" (*SJ*, 165), a local character, even though in his fifties he realizes he has entered a dangerous age "for all men, and especially for one like me who has a tendency to board sinking ships . . . the man of fifty [recognizes] only different kinds of defeat" (*SJ*, 15, 16).

He feels the loneliness of the exile and with his friends at the Bandung Bar recognizes "the legion of the lost . . . lost old men, vagrants huddled around a fire" (*SJ*, 68, 64). In other men he sees the lost soul "seeking cover in a Chinese shop, consoling himself with clubby fantasies and the fact that he was too far away to be of concern, an alien at a great distance, the bird of passage" (*SJ*, 37). Like so many exiles, Jack often feels like one of the kind of "travellers who never arrive, who do not die but are lost and never found . . . alone and among strangers who mock what they can't comprehend . . . who was lost long before he died (*SJ*, 81).

Racism underlies most transactions, social and otherwise, in Theroux's Singapore, from "the completely Chinese flavour of vice" (*SJ*, 124) to "the enactment of the white bachelor's fantasy . . . to be alone with the exotic oriental girl in a ceremonial state of undress" (*SJ*, 125). Jack Fiori works for Chop Hing Kheng Fatt, Ship Chandlers and Provisioners. Because he is white, "I drank in clubs and bars where 'Asians,' as they were called, were not allowed . . . in the end this simple fact of racial exclusiveness landed Hing with many contracts for supplying European ships" (*SJ*, 92). The Chinese move in gangs and family clans and resent the *ang mohs* (Western redheads), who "made the girls vicious," although according to Jack "the girls (who nearly always hated the men they slept with) were improved by their contact with Europeans, quiet undemanding men, unlike their sadistic woman-hating counterparts in the States" (*SJ*,

102). In any case the Chinese use Jack "as Hing, to get Europeans, who didn't haggle and who would pay a few dollars more. The Chinese were after the *ang moh* trade, and it seemed as if I was the only supplier" (*SJ*, 101). Racism surfaces as well between black and white Americans at one of Jack's more triumphant brothels, a legacy of the shadowy and self-destructive American presence in Vietnam.

Jack goes to the airport to pick up William Leigh, an accountant, who has been sent from Hong Kong to audit Hing's books. He and Leigh share their fantasies of the future, the former hoping for money and a yacht, the latter setting his sights on a cottage in Wiltshire in England. Leigh, however, suddenly dies, and on a hot day the funeral is held at a local crematorium. Jack, having told Leigh so much about himself, finally feels only relief: "I was allowed all my secrets again, and could keep them if I watched my step. It was like being proven stupid and then, miraculously, made wise" (*SJ*, 73).

In part 2 Jack in response to Leigh's sudden death and that death's intrusion upon his own middle-aged life, recalls his past. He first worked for his father, a tailor, and then spent the Korean War in Oklahoma. As a freshman at thirty-five he went to college on the G.I. Bill, got mixed up in the beatnik scene of his younger friends, "trying to set them straight on Ezra Pound, who was a fake poet but a genuine fascist" (*SJ*, 107), was charged with possessing drugs, jumped bail, fled to Los Angeles, and sailed to Hong Kong. At thirty-nine be jumped ship and became a hustler in Singapore.

In Singapore Jack discovered that Hing could supply anything at short notice. Hing hired him, and Jack accepted, since he could get a visa only from Hing. On the night of a Sumatra (a wild August storm) Jack managed to ferry twenty-three Chinese and Malay girls out to a British ship in the harbor. His reputation for deliveries was assured, the other Chinese used him as their only white supplier, and his and Hing's business thrived.

At last Jack opens his own brothel, "Dunroamin'," complete with a palm court orchestra: "if my whorehouse was a scale model of the imperial dream, I justified my exploitation by adding to it humour and generous charity, and by making everyone welcome" (*SJ*, 138). Of course, success cannot last. Thugs from one of the secret Chinese societies move in, kidnap and tattoo him as a warning to other interlopers in the trade, and burn "Dunroamin' " to the ground.

Jack becomes an institution in Singapore, sought out by tourists, but he hustles only intermittently, believing that sex should be "slightly masked . . . unhurried, private, imaginative and inexpensive . . . celebrating fantasy [and not] the anonymous savagery of the new pornography, the new cruel sort" (*SJ*, 158). At this point Edwin Shuck, who works for the American Embassy, hires Jack to run "Paradise Gardens," a place for American soldiers to relax and unwind from Vietnam. Hing caters, Jack's cronies hang out there; it becomes a successful tropical hotel, until Shuck suddenly closes the place down.

In part 3 we return to the present, to the crematorium where William Leigh's body has just been incinerated. Jack decides to return to see Edwin Shuck, who wants him to spy on Major-General Andrew Maddox: "Now *you're* going to pimp for him" (*SJ*, 198). Shuck promises Jack ten thousand dollars for the job, and Jack sets up a hotel room to watch Maddox frolic with one of Jack's girls. Jack, however, refuses to give the pictures he takes of Maddox's transactions to Shuck, deciding that even he cannot stoop to blackmail to make a fast buck: "I was a person of small virtue," he explains. "Virtue wasn't salvation, but knowing that might be." "So you're trying to save yourself!" Shuck exclaims. " 'And you, too', I said" (*SJ*, 221).

Jack wanders off into the night, meets a woman in a white dress and blesses the "children with bright lanterns . . . wishing them well with a nod." He concludes that "I was no exile. . . . Fortune might be denied me, but that denial still held a promise like postponement. . . . 'Lady, I've got all the time in the world,' I said, and a high funny note of joy, recovered hope, warbled in my ears as I pronounced this adventurous sentence" (*SJ*, 223).

It is his meeting with William Leigh that prompts Jack Fiori to reassess his life and examine his dwindling prospects. Leigh epitomizes age and death, and in his "white horror-struck expression" at the moment of death, Jack apprehends Leigh's sudden "ability to see far, and see at that great distance something looming, a throng of terrors" (*SJ*, 59). Jack is beginning at fifty-three to recognize those terrors as well and sees in Leigh a "version of myself. . . . His shadow obscured my way; I wanted him to go. . . . Middle age is a sense of slipping and decline, and I suppose I had my first glimpse of this frailty in Leigh" (*SJ*, 49). The notion of a final nothingness dogs Jack's every step in the wake of Leigh's sudden demise, as if part of him had died with Leigh, as if his only true double could be a roasted corpse.

The Singapore Jack inhabits has "an air of ramshackle permanency common in Eastern ports, as if, having fallen so far, they would fall no further" (*SJ*, 25). He is surrounded by decline and decay in the ruined garden of the Bandung, where the sight of palm trees no longer suggests "a graceful symbol of wealth" (*SJ*, 46), and in the brothel at Muscat Lane, "smelling of sharp perfume and the dust of heavy curtains . . . holding many boisterous ghosts and having a distinct shabbiness" (*SJ*, 115). Singapore, is "like something out of a myth" (*SJ*, 126), one of Jack's friends suggests, but it is finally Jack who is the myth, rising within and above historical decay in his almost limitless American faith.

Like the best of American romantics, Jack "would not be burdened by [his] history" (*SJ*, 81). For him poverty holds ultimate promise: "Being poor was the promise of success; the anticipation, a fine conscious postponement made the romance . . . [even] denial still held a promise" (*SJ*, 77, 222). What steers him is an American faith in ultimate rescue, a sense of unbounded luck and adventure, of notions of sudden wealth, fame, and escape: "I was converted to buoyancy . . . The hopeful mutual rescue . . . was the aim of every white bachelor then in the East" (*SJ*, 98, 100). This "visceral longing for success" (*SJ*, 79) underlies all his actions, so much so that circumstances and historical consequences can only temporarily block his progress. His limitless vision rests on his American white male faith in mythic renewal, hope, and rebirth.

Jack's American consciousness differentiates him from his cronies and the others who surround him. He is the practical visionary, the ever-hopeful rascal who fits a cripple for a brace, panders to the men who seek his girls, and carries with him a "faith in extraordinary kinds of rescue, miraculous recoveries" (*SJ*, 37). The images the Chinese thugs have tattooed on his skin reveal "a dripping dagger on my left wrist, a crucifix on my right, [a kind of] convenient symbology" (*SJ*, 152) that suggests both his dangerous life and his faith in an ultimate, and repeatable, resurrection. He believes in no dogmatic religion but often prays and thinks of holiness as a "friendly human act . . . defining virtue as joy and grace as permission granted" (*SJ*, 70). His relief after Leigh's death, the feeling of having been stupid and then being made suddenly wise again, strikes him as a revelation of renewal.

Dreaming of letters written to him, filled with expectations realized and fantasies fulfilled, he yearns for "tangible grace" and utters his litany "which began *Sir Jack, President Flowers, King John,* and so forth. And why stop at King? *Saint Jack!*" (*SJ,* 79). He shepherds his venereal flocks, "keeping those already astray happy and from harm, within caution's limits . . . it was as close to a Christian act as that sort of friendly commerce could be" (*SJ,* 122). Other people's suckers are his souls: "My small virtue was a fidelity to other people's passion, but I would not martyr myself for it, I expected some payment. . . . I took blame, I risked damnation, I didn't cheat" (*SJ,* 126). His is a "saintly testimony" (*SJ,* 126) of a kind, rescued by his free-wheeling sense of humor and forthright descriptions of his plots, schemes, and inner thoughts.

"Dunroamin' " becomes "my little mission-station" (*SJ,* 137), and he sees himself only half playfully as "the kind of angel I expected to visit me" (*SJ,* 140). He appreciates sex as a celebration of fantasy and desire and recalls "the tragic suggestion I saw in their nakedness" (*SJ,* 134) of a couple he once saw in a pornographic film. Conversation suggests "hectic prayer," and he enjoys "my priestly vocation" (*SJ,* 171) while administering to the troops at "Paradise Gardens." His crew become "ragged disciples" (*SJ,* 205), and in refusing to go through with Shuck's plan of blackmail, he pronounces himself once more renewed and reborn: "I had had my nose pressed against two fellers, one dead, one alive. I knew them, and my betrayal, begun exclusively as a crime—I had insisted on that—had ended as an act of faith, the conjuring trick that fails you when you understand it. . . . So I was saved" (*SJ,* 222). It is shortly thereafter that he blesses the "children with bright lanterns."

Jack's faith is as blasphemous in strictly Christian terms as is the American faith in itself and self-reliance, but in *Saint Jack* Theroux presents that faith in its enlightened, self-sufficient buoyancy. It is the saintly testimony of an aged Huck Finn, of a "cheerful rascal, someone greatly ignorant" (*SJ,* 103), who cannot and will not sink into the despairs and decay of middle age. Even though at the very beginning of his memoirs he tells us, "being slow to disclose my nature is characteristic of me" (*SJ,* 9), the disclosures eventually surface, leading the reader onward through this effervescent, first-person narrative.

Jack transcends the querulous and wittily soulless rebelliousness of Waldo, the downtrodden victimization of Sam Fong, the arrogant posturing of Alfred Munday, and the naive missionary zeal and subsequent disillusion of Calvin Mullet. He is probably Theroux's most joyous character, an adventurous, unpretentious soul assured only of his poverty and procrastination as promises of some ultimate reward. Later characters will darken in their assessment of the world and of the American consciousness within it, but Jack proclaims his own sainthood gleefully, and we as readers can only help confirm his buoyant prophecies.

The Family Arsenal (1976): "This Is the Tempest Long Foretold"

Valentine Hood, the main character of *The Family Arsenal,* presents a much darker version of the American consciousness than Jack Fiori. As an American consul in Vietnam, his first overseas post, he has punched the government's minister of defense, made himself a passport, and escaped to London, after being immediately suspended by the ambassador and ordered back to Washington: "It had been a short career, but . . . he had seen the whole world's damaged soul. He considered himself one of Vietnam's last casualties."[3] When the novel opens, the authorities are still looking for him, but Hood has become part of a murky terrorist underground in London, biding his time, waiting for some kind of significant action to pull himself together again: "He craved the kind of blame that would release him honorably from the charge of inaction, a guilt like grace. . . . He closed his eyes and saw . . . a man with no country, unknown among strangers, who had rid himself of his family and who, at that distance, had fallen silent and ceased to act. A calm fugitive: he ridiculed the notion of exile—in this world there was no exile for an American" (*FA,* 18, 225).

Hood realizes that "to live abroad was to create a mythology about yourself, more than a new personality, a liberating fantasy you could believe in, a new world" (*FA,* 226), and yet his fantasy produces only a sullen and smoldering sense of outrage, undirected, waiting for some decisive action or rebellious act, something to transcend "your consul act—the big, cool, noncommittal thing" (*FA,* 157). He knows how violence and intention can lead to unexpected and disastrous results, in his references to Verloc's inadvertently blowing up his simple-minded brother-in-law in Joseph Conrad's *The Secret Agent,* a book which shares the decayed urban slums and atmosphere of a terrorist underground with *The Family Arsenal.* We have come a long way from Saint Jack's buoyant faith and rejuvenating hopefulness, having passed through Alfred Munday's darker fears and guilts.

Hood gets his chance, when he murders Ron Weech, a cruel braggart of a thug, who when he is drunk one night attacks a streetsweeper in the presence of the streetsweeper's small son: "Hood seethed . . . and the boy looked on, helplessly, at his helpless father, as the man struck, slapped him (*Dad!*), nearly losing his balance" (*FA,* 8). Hood follows Weech to a pub and tells him about a stolen painting he is involved with and the opium he can easily get. Weech flashes money, talks tough, describes his betting at the dog races, and informs Hood about some Arab guns and ammunition. Hood has had enough, jumps Weech outside and breaks his neck.

The consequences of Weech's murder prove far murkier than Hood could have expected. Hood spies on Weech's widow, Lorna, and her son, Jason, and in sneaking into Weech's house to return his wallet discovers heaps of stolen merchandise and Sten guns and is himself discovered by Lorna Weech. Realizing that he may have stumbled into some labyrinthine terrorist plot, he moves the guns and merchandise to his house, visits Ralph Gawber (the accountant whom he encountered along with Weech that fateful night at the pub) to set up an account for Lorna, from which money will be sent to her every week, and gradually falls in love with his victim's widow: "Murder had brought him to the widow. . . . The guilt he saw in her intensified his own. . . . She trusted Hood in a hopeless way . . . resigned to his attentions, like an orphan taken up by a strange parent. . . . [His] desertion would ruin her" (*FA,* 92). Caught in unexpected circumstances—"His victim's wife was his victim" (*FA,* 172)—the widow and, unknown to her, her husband's killer smoke opium together, gradually depending more and more upon each other's presence.

One evening Hood and Lorna venture out to the dog races. Willy Rutter, one of Weech's connections and a thug as brutal as he, discovers them there and attacks Hood, who is barely rescued by one of his own sidekicks. Hood has told Lorna that he is a friend of Weech's, but the attack on him raises doubts about him in her mind. Hood, following out the developing connections of conspiracy, later finds Lorna at her home, having been attacked by Rutter's thugs searching for the arms. The upshot finds Hood and Lorna together, fleeing London with Hood's sidekick Murf. "I'll stay with you," Hood assures her, "until you chase me away . . . until you're safe." "I don't even know you," she replies. "Who are you?" (*FA*, 295). But by this time their mutual feelings for each other dissolve any real interest in their past lives.

As the novel develops, Hood begins to recognize the fuller implications of murdering Weech. In killing Weech he feels he has killed the worst in himself, as if he has undertaken a kind of personal exorcism: "Ridding [Lorna's] life of those bastards would rid him of that part of his own past that now seemed a moment of uncontrolled fury, when murdering her husband he had murdered the worst in himself" (*FA*, 231). And yet in planning to murder Rutter and his henchman, he recognizes the fact that "Weech had brought him to it, and he had had to become Weech to complete his revenge" (*FA*, 289). Still he must play out the drama that his killing of Weech has initiated. Even knowing that "to act . . . was to involve himself; no act could succeed because all involvement was failure; and love, a selfish faith, was the end of all active thought" (*FA*, 263); even knowing all of that in his best pessimistic and philosophical manner, yet "he sought to conclude the act he had begun on impulse that summer night. He wished to release himself with a single stroke that would free him even if it left him a cripple" (*FA*, 263).

Hood comes to realize that "it's pride that makes you think you can fight someone else's battles—in Africa, southeast Asia, here, wherever," a shock of recognition that harbors all kinds of implications for America's actions in the later half of the twentieth century, "because it's their weakness that involves you" (*FA*, 266), but once the die is cast, he sees it through, a decision that does not eradicate his past actions—he is still a fugitive at the novel's end—but that sets his own heart and mind straight, that completes the darker consequences his original dark act of murder has generated.

In such a morally murky world no action can remain pure and untainted. Hood's murdering Weech sets in motion a train of consequences that disrupts terrorists' schemes, leads to other murders, and results in an apocalyptic explosion and escape. Weech was the London agent for Willy Rutter's outfit that supplied guns and ammunition to the Provos, a terrorist gang led by Sweeney. The plot becomes more complicated, when Hood is asked by the Provos, through Mayo, his lover and one of the young terrorists who lives with him in southeast London, to make up a counterfeit passport for a Provos agent, the actress Araba Nightwing. Hood's forging the passport will be his entry into the Provos' operation and prove both his abilities and his loyalties to that group. More connections reveal themselves, when Hood learns that Mayo is really named Sandra and is married to the Provos' leader Sweeney, a man with a missing hand who speaks in the "strangled accent of Ulster" (*FA*, 207).

While Hood becomes involved with Lorna Weech, Mayo/Sandra has stolen a valuable painting which she hopes to have ransomed. She mails strips of it with ransom notes, but no one responds. The painting turns out to belong to Lady Susannah Arrow, a wealthy collector and soulless creature, who is pursuing Brodie, the second terrorist who lives with Hood, a girl of sixteen, in her determined lesbian manner. Murf, the adolescent bomb-maker, who is the third person living with Hood, later steals the painting and presents it to Hood as a surprise, when the two of them with Lorna and her son Jason prepare to flee from the city. Hood, however, drops the painting, when he is fleeing from the cemetery where Sweeney has pursued him to kill him. One of Rutter's henchmen, instead, kills Sweeney.

Theroux delights in creating the many characters involved in conspiracies and a kind of low-level espionage. Their world remains a world of violence, murder, assault, bombings, illegal weapons, and intrigue. And the violence leads to other people, other connections, the strange creatures of an urban terrorist underground.

Murf and Brodie are Hood's adolescent roommates. Murf is a bat-faced Cockney boy who wears an earring and makes bombs. Brodie has planted a bomb at Euston Station, displays tattoos, and was rescued from anorexia by Murf, who then introduced her to Hood. Together they make noisy love. It is Brodie who takes Murf to Lady Arrow's house, and it is Lady Arrow who in following Brodie to Hood's house discovers her stolen painting there. In the end Brodie goes to live with Lady Arrow, when Hood's "gang" breaks up.

The third terrorist living with Hood, his bedmate, is Mayo: Hood "had met Mayo at Ward's in Piccadilly in the late spring soon after he arrived. She was drunk; she told him, a perfect stranger, of her plan to steal the painting. . . . He had spent the night with her and at last moved in and tutored her in caution. They agreed to work together" (*FA*, 46). Mayo in her mid-thirties remains evasive and vanishes for long stretches at a time. As Sweeney's wife, she is constantly on the lookout for Provos' prospects, and when Hood at last decides to break up his house, she returns to Sweeney. Hood and Murf, however, rig the house to explode, leaving the stolen merchandise and weapons there to lure Rutter and his gang to their deaths, Mayo returns to retrieve her stolen painting just as Rutter and his henchmen enter, and the bomb goes off.

Lady Susannah Arrow is one of Theroux's most interesting characters. Arrogant and standing well over six feet tall, she takes up people and causes like the latest fads and wishes to make them her own by possessing them completely. "She was a proprietress of fame" who despises the middle class and sees a kind of "simplicity of feeling" between those with great wealth like herself "and the distress of poverty" (FA, 78). To her the middle class remains "selfish, predatory, unprincipled, artless, exposed and lacking any warmth; drooling and cowardly in the most wolfish way. They were the mob—the accountants in Lewisham" (FA, 79). Her ravenous appetites know no bounds: "She made no distinction between friends and lovers, men and women: she slept with both . . . she recruited them, broke them in with sexual tutoring, then paraded them at her lunch parties" (FA, 80). In her self-enclosed secure existence, she longs for the intrigue and conspiracies of her terrorist causes: "She had improved on Bakunin—using privilege to rid herself of privilege. She wished for others to do violence to her wealth and yet to have her own say in their acts. . . . She wished to be both terrorist and the terrorized" (FA, 189).

Arrow's rival is Araba Nightwing, the actress, intent on banning Punch and Judy shows, who despises what she vaguely refers to as "the system" (shades of 1960s banners and slogans) and works with her group, the Purple League, a band of Trotskyites, described by her as "a grassroots movement of workers, the only viable alternative to the existing power structure of hacks and exploiters" (FA, 196).

The link between many of these extraordinary characters turns out to be a tired, decent, middle-class accountant—the type Arrow despises—named Ralph Gawber, who is an accountant for both Arrow and Nightwing and, for a short time, Hood. He lives in southeast London with his wife Norah—a son lived only twelve hours thirty years ago—where he secretly hopes for and fears an apocalypse: "It would serve them right . . . those hot lazy mobs made him wish for a cleansing holocaust—some visible crisis, black frost combined with an economic crash" (FA, 35). It is the middle-class version of revenge against all those who are not as hard-working and as decent and upstanding a citizen as he. He looks out on a world that is "deranged," where "the news was written in blood" (*FA*, 38). He worries about England, remembers some lines from Kipling: "let no star / Delude us—dawn is very far. / This is the tempest long foretold . . . the storm, is near, not past" (*FA*, 108). Catastrophe haunts him; war "had shaped him"; he foresees "a sudden airless fissure, streaking across the grass [and recognizes] a ripeness that was next to decay—the seasons' warning" (*FA*, 160).

At the end of the novel Gawber goes to Hood's house, since Hood has canceled his orders at the bank involving Lorna Weech (Hood is already planning his escape with her), to ask him if there will be any further instructions. He enters, finds no one at home, and leaves, just before Rutter and his henchman arrive. Mayo is already inside searching for the stolen painting. It is Gawber who witnesses the explosion that destroys the house: "The explosion reached him as a muffled roar. . . . The sky was lit. . . . He thought: home, Norah, and tonight Peter Pan [the play Araba Nightwing is starring in]. It is the end of my world. He put his hand to his eyes and tried to stop his tears with his fingers" (*FA*, 281).

Throughout the novel Theroux describes this underground ter-rorist labyrinth as a kind of family: "They were all related . . . it was as if by degrees [Hood] was waking to the true size of his family and seeing it as so huge and branched it included the enemy. To harm any of them was to harm a part of himself. A family quarrel: if he cut them he bled" (*FA*, 204). Mayo and the two adolescents suggest "marriage's parody enacted in a Deptford hide-out that had become a family home" (*FA*, 65). Lady Arrow "saw her role as essentially maternal" (*FA*, 80); and with Gawber at the theater one evening, "allowing the old man to escort him, Hood had experienced a son's cozy serenity" (*FA*, 117). "You see, when I saw that picture in your cupboard I suddenly realized what a family affair this has all become" (*FA*, 149), declares Lady Arrow at Hood's house; Rutter asks Hood: "You one of the family? . . . Because if you're one of the family, then maybe it don't matter" (*FA*, 182, 183). Before Lorna and Hood become lovers, "they were equal, mutually pro-tective, like brother and sister, as if they had shared a parent they both hated, now dead and unmourned" (*FA*, 169).

The family imagery pervades the novel and cuts both ways. On the one hand it works ironically, revealing how disconnected and self-serving all these people really are, how uninterested they are in any mutual benefit or workable scheme to promote some common end. On the other hand certain characters do become more intimate, sharing secrets and hopes and fears with one another in the manner of brothers and sisters, fathers and sons, parents and children. Their antagonisms also express the antagonisms of a family, in which blood is ever so much thicker than water.

Theroux's expression of the modern temper includes anger and outrage, a lashing out at others, as if the family of man were rent by unresolvable divisions, tortured egos, truculent conspiracies, and a smoldering querulous rage in search of the perfect target. The elaborate plot reflects the tentacled reach of large families, both in its interconnectedness and in its incidents of anger and violence. Murf and Brodie feel that "the only way they could possess the city [was] by reducing it to shattered pieces. Exploded, in motion, it was theirs" (FA, 74). Theirs is the modern urge to destroy, attack, disrupt, and defile, bred in the rebellions of the 1960s and early 1970s, appearing in such other Theroux characters as Maude Coffin Pratt, Alfred Munday, Waldo, Marais, and Allie Fox. This anger longs for an apocalyptic cleansing akin to Gawber's visionary hatreds, an attack on the consumerist detritus of modern society, on the modern city itself and the cycle of life it produces.

Theroux's description of the comic apocalypse in the kitchen of Nightwing's play, "Tea for Three," suggests such anger. As kitchen appliances go haywire, the audience hoots with laughter: "They were acting out their strength, celebrating their petty hatred. But the worst of this malice was the acceptance of things as they were, the assumption of oily foreigners, the assumption of greed, the assumption of funny little England. That and the moronic display of food—stacked, burned, thrown about—which titillated the audience like naked flesh. Hood saw it as the coarsest pornography—hunger's greedy ridicule" (FA, 121). In such passages Theroux reinforces the terrorists' hatred of middle-class values, as if he were getting back at Medford, Massachusetts, the consuming "normalcy" of the 1950s, the contemporary values of materialism and acquisition, and his own family's background. It is as if he identifies in part with the terrorists' impulse to destroy or at least disrupt such values, as if the terrorists' arsenal is indeed a family affair, symbolizing the kindred sentiment of all of us locked into industrial societies, crowded cities, and quasi-decadent (because ultimately self-serving and self-indulgent) "life-styles."

Theroux's South London reveals only decay and despair. Deptford reeks of "smoke, silence, emptiness and slow decay, an imperceptible leaching that was a strong smell before it was a calamity" (*FA,* 220). The river suggests "a dead serpent[;] London lay on a plain, the humps and spires showing in dim aqueous light, yellow distances like a burnt-out sea drenched and smoldering under a black sky" (*FA,* 31). Gawber's neighborhood in Catford "had moved into a phase of decline that was, even now, unchecked . . . it would never improve . . . the warm weather . . . started the poisons in bricks and woke the smell of decay" (*FA,* 33, 34-35).

The hill where Hood disposes of Weech's body, "a blankness that might have been labelled *Unexplored* or *Here Live Savages,* was sealed from view in the huge exposed city, as neatly hidden as if it were an island that lay under the sea, the ultimate hiding place" (*FA,* 19). Perhaps this suggests the mysterious hidden depths of each person, of each isolated consciousness, despite the surrounding detritus and violence associated with contemporary existence. From this solitary perspective the self looks out on a world that shifts and changes, as the stolen painting by Rogier van der Weyden suggests.

Throughout the novel Hood eyes the painting from different angles of vision. The self-portrait of van der Weyden at first suggests "an unwilling exile" (*FA,* 44) and later exudes a kind of contentment. Outside the window in the portrait Hood discovers a riot. The face also suggests "a fabulous villain in black . . . a patrician gentleman gleaming with wealth . . . an anxious bridegroom pausing at the window of experience [and in] a split second of calm . . . it was, passionately, a man of action" (*FA,* 100). In suggesting so many characters to Hood, "It shone on him. Its greatness lay in the way the cubes of color gathered to match his own mood . . . it exalted the eye. It shimmered with certainty, it was the surest vision, an astonishing light . . . the only solace he had received, this illumination" (*FA,* 151). Finally, "he knew the face in the self-portrait now: it was the man he had killed, months ago, and he had become that man" (*FA,* 285).

In such an evil world art yet triumphs and sustains, and through it, all men become one, creatures of some exalted communion partaking of some moment of grace freely and mysteriously conferred, true family members in their appreciation, however distorted and uncertain, of "cubes of color," astonishing lights, and artful illuminations. Such power cannot be easily destroyed by all the gasworks and power stations and poisoned rivers in existence. It remains "the ultimate hiding place."

The Family Arsenal breeds conspiracies, double crosses, betrayals, connections, and coincidences that continue to generate larger conspiracies and betrayals, revealing a labyrinth of characters, connections, and subplots that mirror and reflect one another. "Their opiates were plans, plots, counterplots, circular strategems . . . threat and plot replaced action" (*FA*, 98), Hood concludes in assessing the spirit that drives so many of these second-rate subversives.

Theroux cuts back and forth from character to character, from emblematic encounter to emblematic encounter, so that each one crosses another's path unwittingly, while the author slowly ties the noose around them all and links them in an ultimate web of action and reaction, cause and effect beyond their own control. Opium that Hood and Lorna smoke, for instance, turns up in Norah Gawber's medicine, a coincidence, of course, but planting the suggesting that several of these characters are drugged with their own dreams and/or evasions. Gawber's connections to all the characters link their fates together in surprising ways, leading to surprise encounters between Gawber, Nightwing, and Arrow, for instance, at Hood's house.

The intricate structure of the novel mirrors the juxtaposition and crosscutting between characters, indicating how firmly Theroux is in control of his material. The five chapters in part 1, for instance, are carefully arranged: we meet Hood in chapter 1, Gawber in chapter 2; Hood and Gawber meet in chapter 3; Gawber returns home, disconcerted and puzzled, in chapter 4; Hood returns home in chapter 5. In part 2 the web tightens. Part 3 remains more or less a holding action, involving the encounters and relationships between Hood and Mayo, Hood and Arrow, until Hood and Lorna are savagely attacked by Willy Rutter and his gang at the dog track. Part 4 ushers in Hood's meeting with Sweeney and his plans to get Rutter by rigging his house with a bomb. And in part 5 the house explodes, Mayo is killed, Gawber witnesses the explosion, Sweeney is gunned down, and Hood, Lorna, Murf, and Jason hightail it out of London on a train in hopes of making it eventually to Guatemala.

The Family Arsenal reveals a mature Theroux totally in command of his art. At times the coincidences overwhelm the text; the reader can occasionally get lost in all the intricate maneuverings, but the sense of conspiracy that broods over the novel is meticulously and eerily rendered. Theroux does not miss a step in pursuit of this labyrinthine London, this "concealing city" (*FA,* 292). Revenge may suggest redemption of a kind, but we are left unsettled. Where will escape lead to? Murf asks Hood on the train what they will do, when they get to Guatemala. Hood puffs on Murf's cigarette and replies quietly, "Smoke . . . Smoke and tell lies" (*FA,* 296). The family arsenal moves on.

Picture Palace (1978): "Both Cannibal and Missionary"

"I had always chosen opposites," declares Maude Coffin Pratt, the cantankerous, feisty, vulgar, septuagenarian photographer in her memoirs, the landscape of Theroux's ninth novel: "The old when I was young, the blind when I'd valued my eyes, the black and the bizarre when I'd felt white and ordinary."[4] She grew up with "a precocious grasp of bright symmetries. I loved what was beautiful; I knew I was not" (*PP,* 49). "I had always believed that I had been fascinated by double images," she adds (*PP,* 318).

Those double images and those bright symmetries, all the talk about art and life, and Theroux's delight in paradox, overwhelm *Picture Palace,* and in their schematic patternings emerge like cue cards throughout the novel, undermining what should be an exploration of the visual and the concrete, emphasizing the textual and the general. Despite the novel's richness—and Theroux extends his grasp to explore wider subjects and newer territories—Maude remains a voice in a vacuum, a brooding, crotchety presence who reduces all other characters to stick figures and examples of her theorizing.

Paradox and doubleness underlie all things. A lover becomes "both cannibal and missionary, touched with every emotion except doubt" (*PP,* 53). "To be famous is to be fixed. . . . To be fixed is to be dead, and so fame is a version of obscurity" (*PP,*335). A picture palace refers both to the windmill where Maude has stashed her photographs and to her own mind and memory: "The picture palace on the lawn held half the story, but the mind had its own picture palace, much grander. . . . The windmill held my photos and the picture palace of my imagination another set, a different version of the past" (*PP*, 46, 306). Memory holds only "fragments and double exposure, and not one clear picture but an endless roll of blurs" (*PP*, 73). The past interferes with the present.

Art and life battle it out to a draw; one steals from the other; they each reveal and conceal one another. "With the pictures I was two people," Maude insists, "the photographer, the person. Without them, I was no one" (*PP*, 321). So then, "My life was in my pictures" (*PP*, 4). But not really: "how simple my art had been, compared to the endless complexity of my life . . . my work . . . was the least important thing about my life" (*PP*, 275, 307). In fact, "photography was something that rid me of images by disposing of the visible world, a lonely occupation that made me lonelier" (*PP*, 192). Therefore: "my life and work: they were separate, contradictory [even though] my life mattered more than my work, but my work gave no hint of this" (*PP*, 105, 47). In finding art she loses the love of her brother, Orlando, which she hoped her success as a photographer would attract; but, of course, he is really in love with their sister Phoebe, whom Maude describes as "my double . . . I shared their passion. . . . There had been no link between what I was and what I saw" (*PP*, 243).

At one point Maude undergoes a long bout with a kind of psychosomatic blindness that comes upon her when she sees—and then quickly suppresses—her brother and sister making love in the windmill: "I ought to have seen, years ago, that Orlando and Phoebe were lovers. But, then, I'd had only my eyes" (*PP*, 207). Only when she is blind can she truly see: "I came to know that I was inhabiting in my blindness a camera obscura of palatial proportions. I had not lost the visible world; I contained it" (*PP*, 209). As with Oedipus, "blindness had taught me much more about vision" (*PP*, 316).

Paradoxes proliferate. The success of one of Maude's famous pictures, the Lamar Carney Pig Dinner, results in the ruin of her father's reputation and business. Maude insists that observers should drown in her photographs; Orlando and Phoebe, so she surmises, drown themselves when they realize that Maude has discovered their long incestuous affair. "I wanted the viewer to drown among the images without thinking of me" (*PP*, 47), Maude tells us, and in fact that is probably exactly what happened to Orlando and Phoebe. "The best photographers were, to me," she goes on, "like an experience of drowning" (*PP*, 112).

At the heart of *Picture Palace* lies the shadowy Gothic yearning of Maude for her brother Orlando: "We were brother and sister, not a single image but a double creature . . . he was my missing half . . . together, in Orlando and me, I saw perfection: body and soul" (*PP*, 52, 53). They would be "the perfect fit" (*PP*, 147). From such a yearning's perspective, "the camera was only a stratagem to charm him . . . a photograph . . . [was] a feeble duplicate of what I wanted" (*PP*, 57). Of course, "the photography I had taken up as a means of attracting Orlando had itself become an activity that displaced him and helped me forget the heartache I felt for him [even though] I was looking for fame, to win Orlando's love" (*PP*, 93, 95).

Such incestuous longings and images of brothers and sisters permeate the text. Maude hungers for Orlando; Orlando sleeps with Phoebe; Maude regards Phoebe as her double; Kenny and Doris, the "couple" in the pornographic photographs owned by Frank Fusco, the art critic who comes to put together a retrospective exhibit of Maude's art, do what Maude would like to do with her brother. Maude tells Orlando that the brother and sister, Sandy and Blanche Overall, are lovers. Harvey and Hornette, brother and sister, ride bare-assed on horses at the Lamar Carney Pig Dinner. A black man, Teets, tells Maude of having wonderful sex with his sister. Orlando gives Phoebe a copy of William Faulkner's *The Sound and the Fury*, in which brother Quentin exercises incestuous longings for his sister, Caddy Compson, and at last exorcises them by committing suicide.

If the "family" in *The Family Arsenal* created only further conspiracies and entangling betrayals, the Pratt family in *Picture Palace* is regarded by Maude as an "an order," a "faith" (*PP*, 60). It is "like a religion . . . it consoles, it enchants, it purifies. It is roomy seclusion, a kind of sanctified kinship. . . . Many religions attempt, unsuccessfully, to be families, but ours worked . . . we were ancestor-worshippers. We had our own reverences and secrets; we were safe . . . we distrusted everyone else. It was a feast. And it was easy for me to turn these loyalties into desire and not want anything to change; to want it all to last forever just the way it was" (*PP*, 55–56). If the family explodes in *The Family Arsenal*, as if Theroux were overthrowing the machinations of the large family he himself comes from, the family "implodes" in *Picture Palace*, as all three siblings, like some Poesque creatures, tumble into the dark well of incest, two of them eventual suicides—like Roderick and

Madeline Usher in Poe's "The Fall of the House of Usher"?—the
third an estranged and embittered loner, self-enclosed in memories
and recollections, like some querulous ghost haunting her own retrospective, a "coffin" of incestuous paradoxes and chosen opposites.

The Pratts, isolated and wealthy on Cape Cod, seem to require
no one else and spring from other old incestuous families in American
literature. Hawthorne, Melville, O'Neill, Faulkner, and Oates have
conjured them up again and again. Such a "cult," like incest, is
socially destructive, since it turns families in upon themselves and
away from the outside world. It is something most societies regard
as the ultimate taboo. And yet the romantic yearning for complete-
ness, for a total metaphorical identity with another person, permeates American literature and suggests the kind of "bipolarity of
unity," that transcendent longing toward an ultimate harmony in
all things, that our greatest romantic visionary, Ralph Waldo Emerson, described. Theroux is no romantic; his world lies broken and
separate; he sees unity and balance only in paradox, separation, and
opposition. But many of his characters wish otherwise.

In *Picture Palace* polarization and paradox do not cease. Light
suggests both "luminous descent" (*PP*, 158) and distortion, chaos,
lies. It can be kind; it can be cruel. "A quality of light [produces]
that little kick in fiction that tells the truth and makes the rest
plausible" (*PP*, 89), although "light is fickle, unreliable, and lying"
(*PP*, 209). While Maude is blind and invalided at home, "that
barren inactive period was the high point of my career as a photographer" (*PP*, 254) in terms of public recognition and her growing
fame. Her first photos are made from the reversed negatives of blacks
making them look white. In her art she wishes to make the familiar
strange, to capture "surfaces [that] disclosed inner states" (*PP*, 83),
"that stinging second" (*PP*, 64) that would reveal all, using "quaint
arrangements to reveal depths of disturbance" (*PP*, 179).

Maude's is a noble goal, and Theroux describes much of it in the
set pieces within the novel—the descriptions of the photographs:
when they happened, how they happened, what they look like—
but in Maude's constant generalizing about them, she has done to
the book what she had done to a particular photograph: "I had
sucked all the light out of it" (*PP*, 179). Maude once said to Frank
Fusco: " 'The Bible is in error—in the beginning was the picture
or image.' Photography: 'Matter over mind' " (*PP*, 322). In Maude's
memoirs she has not heeded her own pronouncement.

Robert F. Bell associates Theroux's "metamorphoses and missing halves" with mythology and such literary masters as T. S. Eliot and Thomas Mann.[5] The doubling and drowning, he suggests, come from Eliot's *The Waste Land,* as does Maude's association with the blind, androgynous prophet Tiresias. Graham Greene in the novel also suggests a Tiresias figure and appears to Maude as Orlando's double. In the novel Maude comes upon a writer named R. G. Perdew, who looks like and passes himself off as Ezra Pound, another example of the double at work. He has written a novel entitled *Picture Palace;* Perdew rhymes with Theroux; Perdew suggests the French *perdu,* which means "lost."

In Theroux's *Picture Palace,* Bell observes, a man walking down an alley in Boston looks up and sees both Maude and Orlando standing on a fire escape: "Instinct told him we were brother and sister . . . a dream of love, charming and indivisible . . . and as long as he dreamed of us I would love Orlando" (*PP,* 52). (Orlando also happens to be the name of the transsexual character in Virginia Woolf's novel, *Orlando.*) This scene, Bell asserts, parallels another in Thomas Mann's *Felix Krull,* in which Krull the con-artist, obsessed with double images, discovers a brother and sister on a balcony. Krull reflects: "the beauty here lay in the duality, in the charming doubleness. . . . Dreams of love . . . they were of pri-Mal indivisibility and indeterminateness."[6]

For Bell "magic transformation or metamorphosis, blindness, androgyny, the double image, longing for the union of the brother-sister pair, and interchangeability of identities" link Theroux to Eliot, Mann, and Ovid; Theroux "has come to terms with the literary masters of the past and put them to use in his own work by showing us their portraits and cunningly mounting segments of their work in his photomontage."[7] However clever the argument, the mounting repetitions of doubling and redoubling still overwhelm the text and reduce narrative to signpost, memoir to message, an act curiously out of character for such a supposedly famous and well-regarded photographer.

Even the structure of the plot itself turns on the doubling of revelation: Maude's initial discovery of Orlando and Phoebe making love in the windmill, which brings on her blindness, and Maude's discovery of the photograph of that event, which leads to her story of Orlando's and Phoebe's double suicide by drowning. Early in the novel she comes upon her brother and sister springing up out of

the grass, "Phoebe in her white dress . . . Orlando kneeling in-
nocently . . . and in the foreground a mass of fallen apples like
the windfalls on the morning after a storm" (*PP*, 62). Those fallen
apples obviously suggest anything but innocence.

At the end of part 3 Maude discovers her siblings' sexual secret:
"He was on his knees, the veins standing out on his forehead, marble
and blood, in a posture of furious pagan prayer, his mouth fixed in
demand. There were clawmarks on his shoulders . . . he looked
so tormented. His reflection blazed on the floor, a white shadow
struggling under him, his double heaving at him" (*PP*, 201). Maude
shudders: "they were one . . . and I was blind" (*PP*, 202). She
keeps her dark secret in the darkness of her blindness. Toward the
end of the novel Maude stumbles across the photograph of that exact
same moment between Orlando and Phoebe. In fact, she describes
the photograph she discovers among those of Kenny and Doris in
Frank Fusco's drawer in exactly the same way: "He was on his knees
. . . his double heaving at him" (*PP*, 323). She cannot, however,
remember how the picture had been taken, but its "drowning quo-
tient" staggers her, as she "pitched forward into one of my own
photographs" (*PP*, 325).

Immediately, as if entranced, she envisions Orlando and Phoebe
plotting their double suicide in the boat, having discovered the
photograph Maude had taken of them. Even at the moment of their
death Maude wants to feel a part of them, convincing herself that
it was her picture that drove them to it, that she did indeed affect
their lives if only negatively. She wants at least to have been the
cause of their watery coffin, thus sanctifying the grim recognition
of her middle name. Their death frees her, or so she thinks: "The
moment they were lost I broke clean through the surface" (*PP*, 329),
and she goes on to visit the preview in New York of her retrospective,
convinced that "I knew I had driven them into the sea. I had killed
them with a picture" (*PP*, 336). Art can still triumph and affect
lives, however negatively, even though Fusco has left the photograph
of Orlando and Phoebe out of the show. At that show Maude
remains, as she always has remained, "merely a spectator . . . for
the mind was revealed by the way it distorted, or suppressed, or
seized upon a particularly telling travesty" (*PP*, 344).

The plot marches along, peppered with Maude's meetings with
and photographing of various celebrities, many of whom are sketched
in shallow, one-dimensional terms, summed up in a nutshell, and

do not carry the weight and "fullness" that many of the fictional characters do. When Frank Fusco comes to South Yarmouth on Cape Cod to interest Maude in a retrospective show of her art, she flies to London to photograph Graham Greene in perhaps the most successful celebrity encounter in the novel.

Graham Greene reminds Maude of Orlando, and she is intoxicated by his eyes: "They were pale blue and depthless, with a curious icy light . . . with a hypnotist's unblinking blue. His magic was in his eyes, but coldly blazing they gave away nothing but this warning of indestructible certainty" (*PP,* 17). His "blind man's luminous stare" (*PP,* 22) reminds Maude of her blindness a long time ago: "I had the feeling of being with a kindred spirit, a fellow sufferer" (*PP,* 24), an interesting assessment, since he looks to her like her long-dead brother. Greene persuades her to renounce photography, and the sudden appearance of eight Japanese gentlemen, a striking coincidence, since one of Greene's stories is "The Invisible Japanese Gentlemen," convinces her that "they were angels embodying the urgent proof that I write and remember. They were Greene's own magic trick" (*PP,* 29). She fails to take Greene's picture, suffers a heart attack, recovers, and decides to explore the picture palace of her mind and memory, not her art.

In part 2 memory begins. In 1907 at age eleven Maude remembers taking her first photographs, standing her family on their heads. Orlando suggests she should go to New York to try her luck. There she snaps the back of D. H. Lawrence's head, after he tries to seduce her. She opens her first exhibition at the Wharf Theatre in Provincetown with pictures of Paul Robeson and the "Boogie-Men," the black subjects turned white by reversing the negatives of them.

Maude continues to recollect her life and art, recalling her getting in to see Alfred Stieglitz and taking his picture with her new Speed Graphic and her journey to Florida to find her parents wintering at Lamar Carney's Victorian pile in Verona. In Verona she boards with a circus troupe in a local rooming house and snaps her famous photo, "Boarders," followed by sneaking into the infamous Lamar Carney Pig Dinner, a "cannibal feast" for men only, including her father, where the circus performers perform naked. She returns to South Yarmouth, discovers Orlando and Phoebe in the windmill, and is struck blind.

In part 4 the Camera Club in New York discovers Maude's work, waxes ecstatic about her Florida pictures, and in two months she

becomes the new sensation of the photography world. She, meanwhile, festers in the Cape Cod homestead, a blind invalid with a
dark secret. At last she decides to go to New York, disguising her
blindness as best she can, and on a crowded street photographs a
firebug at the scene of a fire by the sounds of his eager snufflings.
Critics worship her at the Camera Club, but she knocks her glasses
off, and they discover her blindness. "The Blind Photographer of
the Cape" is now confined to her family's house.

Suddenly she regains her sight. Orlando returns one evening with
a World War II buddy, Woodrow Leathers, who sneaks into Maude's
bed at night and makes love to her, while she thinks he is Orlando
who at last has come to bed her. More tales of celebrity photos
follow—a series of rooms in which she finds an ornery Frost, a
drunken Faulkner she decides not to photograph, and a "pinched
beaky" Eliot. And in the winter of 1946 she enjoys the great success
of her exhibition at a Mayfair gallery in London. It is then the news
comes of Orlando's and Phoebe's accidental drowning.

In part 5, the final part of the novel, Maude's parents die, her
father of a coronary, her mother of a broken hip and pneumonia;
the mother's last words are, as if encouraging Maude's unveiling
the ambiguous truths of her art and life, "Pull up the shades."
Maude discovers the photo of Orlando and Phoebe among Frank's
masturbation collection, "the only one in fifty years that truly mattered: suppressed! How like a masturbator to hide his imagery in
shame" (PP, 343). The novels speeds to its conclusion—the con-
cocted tale of the double suicide, Maude's visit to her own retrospective in New York, her recognition that she has become, as she
always was, "merely a spectator, stinking of chemicals. I had to be
seen to be believed" (PP, 344).

The engineered neatness of Maude's paradoxes and her fascination
with double images, however, stifle the narrative flow of the text,
slow it down, and produce at last a musing voice in a void, brooding
over itself and trying to tidy up in a dexterously double-edged
manner. As photograph leads on to photograph and memory to
memory, veil leads on to veil, at once being stripped away to reveal
the shock of recognition about Orlando and Phoebe in her life and
at the same time put in place to conceal that shock in her quirky,
clever photographs, consciously subverting family groups, changing
blacks into whites, capturing celebrities at odd angles, standing her
loved ones on their heads. We can never know if Orlando and Phoebe

drowned accidentally or whether they plotted their own suicides. They remain such shadowy, undeveloped characters in any case that they seem more projections of Maude's own mind than flesh-and-blood characters out to avenge or enjoy themselves. They evaporate within the duplicitous cross-examination of Maude's calculating and calculated double vision.

And yet Theroux stretches himself as a writer in *Picture Palace.* He pushes beyond the tight thriller construction of *The Family Arsenal* and beyond the "witchcrafty" Gothic designs of *The Black House.* His playing with a literary text in all its doubleness—as revelation, as concealment, as veil, as photograph—reveals a novelist experimenting at the height of his powers, broadening their scope, and if the novel is not ultimately successful, it certainly looks ahead to the greater one to follow.

Maude may exist in a void, not merely because everyone else in the text remains one-dimensional and shadowy, but because she does not carry enough "mythic resonance" as a character in her own right. As an artist she is full of generalized theories and cranky vulgarities, but these ring hollow, as if she had sprung from her own Platonic conception of herself, not from a solid Yankee background or an American culture. She inhabits her own internal world, where theoretical paradoxes and epithets outweigh the very images and surfaces she supposedly celebrates. The void in the world that surrounds her may be nothing more than her own self-projected void, a mind in search of elegantly spun paradoxes and doublings in its contemplation of itself. Maude's consciousness may carry an aura of self-reliant "Americanness" with it, a kind of Emersonian faith in the self's projections of itself, but the result is more the claustrophobic, coffin-encapsulated world of Poe without Poe's more narcissistic and nightmarish trappings.

If Maude is locked within her own memories and projections, she manages them all very blithely and is left lonely and an outcast but with no real pain or despair. Perhaps Theroux's craft has rescued her in a way she doesn't deserve to be rescued, as if her duplicitous web of life and art, sight and blindness, light and darkness is so meticulously constructed and balanced it nearly vanishes in the plethora of "bright symmetries." Other writers have created such solipsistic characters, such as Henry James in his short story, "The Beast in the Jungle," but these have paid the dark price for their solipsism. Maude rides through on her cranky wit and querulous posturings and, despite some misgivings, remains virtually intact, unscathed, strangely redeemed and restored. Her picture palace— both of them, the pictures and her memories—leaves her thinking of Fusco: "I was home, in my room, drinking alone in my nightie and reflecting that if the pictures were his so was the guilt; and I was at last free" (*PP,* 344).

Maude Coffin Pratt surfaces too easily from drowning in her picture palace. Waldo could manage it by murdering his mistress, but the farcical and satirical tone of that first novel leads the reader to expect and accept anything. The aesthetic void in this book has produced its own moral void, and Theroux's irony is not strong enough to rescue either of them. Maude is too much of a self-redeemed, self-congratulatory character. Her real act of incest may be the book itself in its own incestuous self-renewal and spurious gift of grace.

The Mosquito Coast (1982): "Christ Is a Scarecrow"

We drove past Tiny Polski's mansion house to the main road, and then the five miles into Northampton, Father talking the whole way about savages and the awfulness of America—how it got turned into a dope-taking, door-locking, ulcerated danger zone of rabid scavengers and criminal millionaires and moral sneaks. And look at the schools. And look at the politicians. And there wasn't a Harvard graduate who could change a flat tire or do ten pushups.[8]

We are off, headed for the Mosquito Coast, beginning with this rambling, obsessive tirade, with which Allie Fox dazzles his thirteen-year-old son and idolatrous worshiper, Charlie.

The Mosquito Coast represents the culmination of Theroux's art, complete with the broad scope and themes of *Picture Palace,* the brisk, tight plotting and attack on authority of *The Family Arsenal,* and a character like the querulous curmudgeon of *The Black House.* All of Theroux's art is on display here: the attention to detail, the individual self confronting an alien landscape, the resonances of doubling and symbolic action, the emblematic encounters, the clash between personal illusion and realities, the play of myth and history, the encapsulated self swallowing its own consciousness of the world at the risk of destroying everyone else, the demonic and Gothic overtones that lead to collapse and destruction. And all of this

Theroux expands and explores in terms of the American myths of self-reliance, technological domination, the ruination and praise of nature, and the self as God in the latter half of the twentieth century. As one reviewer put it, " 'The Mosquito Coast' shows a cosmopolitan expatriate novelist pondering his imaginative sources as an American writer, and the relation of those sources to the world as it now seems to be."[9] It is Theroux's finest imaginative fiction.

The structure of the novel, which parallels the journey within, propels the characters along their fated path from revelation to destruction, as if some dark god were seeing to their inevitable destination. Finally they arrive at the Mosquito Coast, which to Allie Fox suggests only death and savages, "the coast of America" (*MC*, 363), but which suggests as well an ultimate psychological landscape and showdown. An adventure tale and quest with such a structure suggests everything from William Golding's *Lord of the Flies* and Joseph Conrad's *Heart of Darkness* to Herman Melville's *Moby-Dick*, Hawthorne's and Poe's probings into darker interiors, and Mark Twain's *The Adventures of Huckleberry Finn.* The journey depicted evokes biblical plagues and calamities, the ravages of fire and flood, like a kind of demented Noah's ark on an apocalyptic ride into hell. And the five parts of the novel emphasize this sequence of discovery and loss from strange towns to stranger rivers, since "in the jungle all rivers are mazes" (*MC*, 179), leading on to darker interiors in that jungle and in the soul: "Banana Boat" leads to "The Icehouse at Jeronimo," and from there the Foxes move out to "Brewer's Lagoon," "Up the Patuca," and finally arrive at "The Mosquito Coast."

Allie Fox, inveterate inventor and megalomaniacal monologist, frustrated after working on Tiny Polski's asparagus farm in Massachusetts, decides to take his family elsewhere. He leads them to Baltimore to board the ship *Unicorn*, but none of them knows where he is taking them. On board the Foxes meet the Reverend Gurney Spellgood and his family, materialistic missionaries secure in their American faith, who are off to Guampu in Honduras to spread the faith, complete with their videocassettes and ice cream. Allie directs the captain of the ship, attempting to usurp his authority during a storm, rails against missionaries in general, goads Charlie into climbing the rigging during the storm, much to the captain's rage, and carries on in his characteristically blustering, bludgeoning manner.

In part 2, "The Icehouse at Jeronimo," the family arrives at La
Ceiba on the coast of Honduras, "a town of dead ends" (*MC,* 109).
Allie buys a small town in the jungle, which he calls "Jeronimo,"
from Mr. Weerwilly, a drunken German: "Now Father was in sole
charge. He had brought us to this distant place and in his magician's
way surprised us by buying a town. . . . I just wanted to be near
him" (*MC,* 114), Charlie the narrator confides. The Foxes embark
for the open sea in Mr. Haddy's launch, sputter up the river Aguan
enclosed by jungle, and come upon a ruined clearing. There they
meet the Ropers, whom Allie misnames the Maywits and who live
in a shack. Work commences with Allie at the helm, employing
the Magwits and the Zambus, the local natives.

Allie builds Fat Boy, a huge "firebox that makes ice." They all
celebrate their first Thanksgiving in August, harvesting beans, the
day after Fat Boy is completed. The children, meanwhile, sneak off
to make their own camp, which they call the Acre: "I liked this
place for its secrecy and best of all because it was filled with things
that Father had forbidden" (*MC,* 168), all those very American,
capitalist things they can imagine, such as stores and spending
money, schoolteachers and telephones.

In order to operate Fat Boy, Allie takes off to get some ammonia
and hydrogen. He then demonstrates Fat Boy's ability to make a
snowball and decides to take some ice "to the hottest, darkest,
nastiest corner of Honduras, where they pray for water and never
see ice" (*MC,* 177). In his new dugout, which he calls "The Icicle,"
he sets out for the jungle village of Seville. Unfortunately, the naked
Indians there have already seen ice, which the missionaries long ago
provided, and fall to their knees to pray over Allie and his arrival:
"*Ah Fadder wart neven hello bead name—*" Needless to say, Allie is
furious, and even more so when on a second visit to Seville, he
discovers the Indians have made a fake Fat Boy and are worshipping
it as an idol.

Dissatisfied, Allie decides to strike deeper into the jungle. He
makes a terrible trip up into the mountains and through dense
jungle to reach the almost nonexistent village of Olancho, trans-
porting an egg-shaped iceberg on a sled. Grim, dirty Indians inhabit
Olancho, and the ice has melted so badly, Allie has put pieces of
it into knapsacks to keep. He shows them a twig of ice, but before
they can see it, it melts in his hand. The Indians are unimpressed
and urge him to leave. Allie discovers three white men in the village

and thinks that they are the Indians' slaves, when in fact the opposite
is true.

Charlie realizes that something is wrong when his father proclaims
that the Indians were "flabbergasted and confounded" by the ice,
and he adds, "What ice?" Allie's lie outrages and confounds Charlie—
"Father's lie, which was also a blind boast, sickened me and separated me from him" (*MC*, 227)—but at the last he does not lie
to Mother when they return. Unfortunately, the Maywits have fled,
and the three white men from Olancho have followed them, in-
tending to take over Jeronimo. Coolly and calmly Allie ushers them
into the bunkhouse, which is none other than Fat Boy, imprisons
them, and freezes them to death, after ordering the other buildings
destroyed. In that apocalyptic moment Fat Boy explodes, and the
family rushes to the Acre to escape the poisoned paradise.

The rest of the novel charts Allie's inevitable downfall, as he
pursues further and further frontiers to conquer and plunges his
family into a megalomaniacal nightmare of mud, tempest, and
disaster. After Jeronimo's destruction, Mr. Haddy suggests they
move to Brewer's Lagoon, and so they pole down the Rio Sico,
arguing openly, and arrive at the low, muddy, incredibly hot and
wasted place, beginning their scavenging for junk to build a home.
Allie meanwhile has announced that America has been destroyed
and sees himself as the great rescuer of his family. Slowly he con-
structs a houseboat out of junk on the bank and proclaims that
Jeronimo should have been destroyed, because it was a mistake
riddled with chemicals. His wife, however, speaks the truth: "Your
garden is imaginary. Your chickens are imaginary. There is no crop.
We haven't planted anything. . . . There's nothing here but trash
from the beach. . . . Look at yourself, Allie. You don't look human" (*MC*, 288).

Mr. Haddy secretly brings Charlie some gasoline and spark plugs
for the houseboat, while Charlie has to insist to his father that he
found them in the mud. After a long period of absolutely no rain,
a huge storm comes and engulfs them, and Allie decides to guide
their boat upriver, away from the Mosquito Coast, deeper into the
jungle: "They're all dying down there, but we're going to live"
(*MC*, 315).

"Up the Patuca" against the current the Foxes head, with Allie
proclaiming that "in all the world we were the last ones left" (*MC*,
321). Jerry, Charlie's eleven-year-old younger brother, who has never

shared his brother's faith in their father's actions, and who has seen
La Ceiba as it actually is in his literal, sharp-eyed manner—"It's
junk, it stinks, it's crappo, I hate it" (MC, 103)—is appalled at
his father's condition after the destruction of Jeronimo. He has been
miserable at Brewer's Lagoon, realizes that "Dad's killing us" (MC,
325), and for his obstinacy and doubt Allie puts him into the dugout
attached at the back of the houseboat: "Then Father cast it off and
let it zoom downriver. Jerry was too terrified to paddle . . . 'That
was insane!' Mother said" (MC, 322, 323). The other children, the
twin girls, Clover, who is "just like father," and April, who is more
easygoing and forgiving like Charlie, are too young to understand
what is going on.

Suddenly the shear pin for the motor falls into the muddy water.
Jerry and Charlie dive to find it, fail in their attempt, and so Allie
plunges overboard. He does not return: "Jerry had stopped looking.
He was staring at me. His face was relaxed—very white and hopeful,
like someone sitting up in bed in the morning" (MC, 329), as if
the nightmare were over. They exult, feel free, until Allie suddenly
surfaces and howls, "Traitors!" Both Charlie and Jerry are exiled to
the dugout.

The Foxes proceed up river and come to Guampu, the village
where the Spellgoods are living. Charlie is pleased to see the village,
the church: "It was all glorious and orderly and clean, a white harbor
among the loopy trees and wild vines, standing straight on this
crooked river" (MC, 344). He goes ashore and discovers the Spellgoods watching the Muppets on television and eating ice cream.
Emily, appalled at how shaggy and disheveled he looks, tells him
that America has not been destroyed. It is the last straw: "And
Father seemed tiny and scuttling, like a cockroach when a light
goes on" (MC, 351).

The novel rushes to its inevitable climax. Charlie and Jerry with
their family plan to escape from Allie. Allie, however, appalled at
the rediscovery of the Spellgoods, blows up their generator and sets
fire to their plane. Charlie tackles him and with Jerry's help ties
him up. As the family is escaping in the dugout, Allie manages to
stand, but Spellgood fires the fatal shot that brings him down. He
remains alive but paralyzed. Mother leads the expedition downriver.

While Allie has been boisterous and manic, mother has remained
calm and silent: "they seemed like a wild man and an angel . . .
plowing through dark water with black jungle on one side and deep

sea on the other . . . an example of the kind of life we led" (*MC*, 123). Slowly her loyalty to her husband falters; she lashes out at him—"You're paranoid . . . you're getting shrill"—and his killing the three white men in Fat Boy proves to be the last straw for her. Sanity takes over, when Mother—she has no other name—leads the family downriver to the Mosquito Coast.

On the Mosquito Coast Allie dies, having witnessed the vultures jerking baby turtles out of their shells when "tossed ashore on [their] back[s] by a rogue wave. . . . Sunlight made this nightmare more horrible" (*MC*, 368). At the very end a vulture swoops down on Allie's corpse "and struck and tore again, like a child snatching something extra because he knows he will be scolded anyway, and this one had his tongue" (*MC*, 370). The family returns to La Ceiba, and Charlie decides that "the world was all right . . . though after what Father had told us, what we saw was like splendor. It was glorious even here, in this old taxicab with the radio playing" (*MC*, 374).

Theroux strengthens his structure with the use of parallels, symmetries, and balances. Three times Allie dares Charlie to perform some potentially dangerous act, supposedly strengthening his emerging manhood, whether it is sitting on a rock in Baltimore waiting for the tide to come in, climbing the rigging of the *Unicorn* (the boat that takes them to Honduras) during the storm at sea, or climbing to the top of Fat Boy at Jeronimo. We already know Theroux's ideas about being a man, which include the commands to "Be stupid, be unfeeling, obedient, soldierly and stop thinking . . . the quest for manliness [is] essentially right-wing [and] puritanical,"[10] notions that would describe Allie sufficiently.

Allie also tells Charlie two major lies, when he describes how excited the Indians were at Olancho to discover the ice he had brought them and when he announces that America has been destroyed. Charlie is outraged by the first and finally disillusioned by the second. Aboard the *Unicorn* Charlie kills a sea gull. "That's bad luck," Emily Spellgood pronounces. And later on at Brewer's Lagoon "Father killed a vulture with a slingshot for no other reason than to show us how the rest of the vultures would feed on it" (*MC*, 285) and, we might add, eventually on him.

Paradoxes, ironies, and confrontations flourish within the text but never overwhelm its brisk pacing and swift narrative power. The missionary Spellgood kills the missionary Fox. Fat Boy makes ice out of fire, a sign perhaps of civilization and technology, and ends up an icy tomb that produces a fiery holocaust. Charlie's faith in his father combats the realistic nightmare he finds himself and his family trapped in. "That's a consequence of perfection in this world," intones Allie, "the opposing wrath of imperfection" (*MC*, 261). He describes an almost Manichean vision that sets him up against a collapsing and unfinished world. The simpler but conventionally social life at the Acre contrasts the one-man show at Jeronimo: "we could do whatever we wanted. We had money, school, and religion here, and traps and poison. No inventions or machines . . . we were in touch with the seasons" (*MC*, 190, 232). Missionaries, supposedly intent on spreading the spirit and the faith, represent the consumer ethic of American materialism, which has spread everywhere and consumed Theroux's vision of the world, complete with "Twinkies and cheese spread in spray cans and crates of Rice-a-Roni" (*MC*, 177). "Mother had said that if [Father] was right [about America's destruction], we were the luckiest people in the world. If he was wrong, we were making a terrible mistake" (*MC*, 334), Charlie reports, and in that double-edged comment nicely sums up the duplicities and resonances of Theroux's carefully crafted text.

Romance crumbles beneath Theroux's sharp and careful eye for detail. At night La Ceiba "was magic . . . under the bright barnacled moon" (*MC*, 103), but in the morning "it was like a nightmare of summer ruin, a town damaged by sunlight" (*MC*, 104). "The view from the ship had been like a picture, but now we were inside that picture. It was all hunger and noise and cruelty" (*MC*, 109).

Allie Fox strides like a colossus, who eventually reveals his feet of clay, at the center of *The Mosquito Coast*. He is inexhaustible, full of inventions and plans, manic, unrelenting, a rampant egotist, despising America's technology yet over-eager to produce his own in the same conquering spirit, a radical humanist who stands at the center of his manufactured universe. He shows no cowardice but launches his campaigns fearlessly and bombastically like the loudest of con-artists eager to dazzle the masses. He is a mechanical genius, the last man, preaching his ultimate faith in himself and in his ideas, using his voice like a weapon: "It was as if Father had created the stream with his speeches, as if he had talked it into existence with the racket and magic of his voice. From will power alone, so it seemed, he had made the pleasant valley appear" (*MC*, 269). He is a cult leader, a sorcerer, a magician full of Yankee ingenuities. "I'm Dr. Frankenstein!" he exclaims, and Charlie agrees: "there was no man on earth more ingenious" (*MC*, 275).

Theroux's bold stroke transforms Allie Fox from mere egocentric inventor into an allegorical figure representing American myth and imagination. In many ways he performs according to Alexis de Tocqueville's description of the philosophical method of the Americans: "To evade the bondage of system and habit, of family maxims, class opinions, and, in some degree, of national prejudices; to accept tradition only as a means of information, and existing facts only as a lesson to be used in doing otherwise and doing better; to seek the reason of things for oneself, and in oneself alone; to tend to results without being bound to means, and to strike through the form to the substance—such are the principal characteristics of what I shall call the philosophical method of the Americans."[11] Fox sees the world as an unfinished place, created by an ineffectual creator: "What a thoroughly rotten job God made of the world! . . . I could give Him a few pointers if He's planning any other worlds. He certainly made a hash of this one" (*MC*, 278, 105). The Bible is only "an owner's guide, a repair manual to an unfinished invention" (*MC*, 7). Such notions lead to the belief that the self alone is God, that romantic faith celebrated in the essays of Ralph Waldo Emerson, which creates a self-reliance that not only rivals but transcends a belief in some absolute, distant God. "Let's face it," Allie says. "[I am] doing a slightly better job than God" (*MC*, 158). "May God forgive you," the Reverend Spellgood intones. "Man is God," Allie retorts. And in plotting to carry his ice deeper into the jungle, he muses, "You feel a little like God" (*MC*, 201).

Allie Fox reflects the great American faith in an ultimate self. As John P. McWilliams, Jr., suggests, the American's energies "are devoted to the process of transformation. . . . Committed to undirected growth, the American can have no lasting identity save the exertion of force, the sheer power of self-creation." He will extend his notions of individualism "into the belief that all knowledge could be found within the self" and will go on to "create the world in his own self-image by projecting his self onto the world." In fleeing American technology and cultural myths, Allie Fox only reproduces them once again in his Honduran clearing, creating his spiritual Walden, his socially hierarchical Brook Farm, his frontier paradise, and his fanatical Xanadu. He will subdue the wilderness in that "sort of cold and implacable egoism"[12] Tocqueville discovered in the dark heart of American society.

When Jeronimo explodes, Allie is excited by the possibility of more space, more wilderness, more area that he can subdue and eventually dominate. Dominated by his own relentless need to make and make again, a kind of "state of psychological becoming without geographical boundary," he presses on in the mud and junk of Brewer's Lagoon, fueled by his own fantasies, driven in his "world of self-making, a state of mind in which, by sheer force of imagination, one could create oneself"[13] and in doing so subdue a world and re-create it in one's own image. Such a ravenous and demonically romantic spirit craves more room, more emptiness in which to live out the ego's devouring fantasies: "He was very restless and hungry-seeming and now less predictable than ever" (MC, 275). In such a state Allie Fox inhabits the monomaniacal territory of such egocentric creatures in American literature as Captain Ahab in Moby-Dick, Thomas Sutpen in William Faulkner's Absalom, Absalom!, Jay Gatsby in Scott Fitzgerald's The Great Gatsby, Hawthorne's mad scientists, doctors, and manipulative magicians, such as Westervelt in The Blithedale Romance, and many more.

The darker aspects of such an ego soon appear. Charlie discovers that his father "was dead set on improving things," but that "he thought of himself first! . . . He liked the odds stacked against him. . . . Selfishness had made him clever. He wanted things his way—his bed and his food and the world as well" (MC, 276, 277). " 'God got bored,' Father said. 'I know that kind of boredom but I fight it' " (MC, 233). As John Irwin makes clear, "With the loss of belief in an external absolute, the self expands to fill the void, but at the moment when the self becomes absolute, at the moment when it sees that everything is a projection of itself, then the self realizes that it has become nothing, that it is indistinguishable, 'a colorless all-color.' "[14] The self has conjured up its own emptiness, its own rampant dissatisfactions and discomforts, and creates in its own image a further emptiness, a world "so wholly solipsistic, so fundamentally dead,"[15] that it can lead only to an escalating fury and a final extinction.

Theroux underlines his notions of Allie Fox with certain symbolic images. For instance, Fat Boy, described as an Egyptian pyramid and "a block of dark marble, a monument or tomb in the jungle"

(*MC*, 171), reminds Charlie of his father: "This was no belly—this was Father's head, the mechanical part of his brain and the complications of his mind, as strong and huge and mysterious. . . . I could see that it had order, but the order—the size of it—frightened me. . . . You could die here, or—trapped inside—go crazy" (*MC*, 160). That connection continues to scare Charlie: "I had seen Father's mind, a version of it—its riddle and slant and its hugeness" (*MC*, 170). And later he remembers his climbing through Fat Boy, realizing that "I had seen just how tangled it was. . . . What he was, he had made. His ravings came out of those orbits and circuits, that teeming closet of pipes and valves and shelves and coils—the ice maker, his brainache" (*MC*, 365). When Fat Boy explodes, "Father had turned away from the blast. One side of his face was fiery, the other black. He had one red eye" (*MC*, 252). Such an image evokes the face of the devil, as witnessed in the nightmarish tar-and-feathering parade in Nathaniel Hawthorne's "My Kinsman, Major Molineux."

Jeronimo itself suggests new worlds and new visions. At Jeronimo people speak a mixture of English, Spanish, and Creole, "so that what came out sounded like a new language" (*MC*, 184), and for Allie Jeronimo can pass through the Iron and Stone Ages quickly, suggesting the passage through all of history's stages: "It'll be 1832 in a few days! By the way, people, I'm planning to skip the twentieth century altogether" (*MC*, 154). When Allie discovers in a trap one day a snake eating a snake, he comments, "There's a perfect symbol for Western civilization" (*MC*, 231), seeing it in Darwinian terms and yet not realizing that the image represented wisdom to the ancients and the symbol of a mystical, circular harmony at the center of the Romantics' self-reliant universe. Such images resonate throughout the novel and increase the fablelike qualities of the book, however briskly conceived in Theroux's realist's manner.

In such a closed egocentric world, which Allie Fox creates, doubling reveals only entrapment, the repetitions and routines of the prison house, the dark mirrors of a nightmare. The Maywits appear to be "our reflections—shrunken shadows of us" (*MC*, 133). "Duppies is your own ghost" (*MC*, 121), explains Mr. Haddy to Charlie, and Mr. Maywit adds, "Everyone got a Duppy. They is the same as yourself. But they is you other self. They got bodies of they own" (*MC*, 147). "The future spoke to Father," Charlie reports, "but for me it was silent and blind and dark . . . the past was the only real thing, it was my hope—the very word *future* frightened me" (*MC*, 343). From fire Allie has produced ice; from his own fiery self-certainty—the mad center of the American myth of self-reliance and the self-made man—he produces destruction and devastation and at last his own death.

Throughout the novel Allie celebrates savages and despises scavengers as part of his personal mythology. "He used the word *savages* with affection. . . . In his nature was a respect for wildness. . . . He seemed both fascinated and repelled by them" (*MC*, 9). Part of his desire to get to the Honduran jungle is both to rescue the savages from the rhetoric and visions of other missionaries and also to dazzle them with his own rhetorical sermons and ice-producing magic. However, he comes to view savagery as the heresy to his own orthodox faith in self-reliance: "Father went on to say that savagery was seeing and not believing you could do it yourself, and that that was a fearful condition" (*MC*, 157). True savagery leads only to the defeat of the imagination, to the static fantasies V. S. Naipaul decried in his own countrymen. "It's savage and superstitious to accept the world as it is," Allie declares. "Fiddle around and find a use for it!" (*MC*, 233).

What Allie has no use for are the scavengers of this world, although as his vision darkens and he becomes more desperate, he describes a hand-to-mouth existence at Brewer's Lagoon as both "like savages [and] like scavengers" (*MC*, 313). Scavengers are like the sea gulls at the town dump back in Massachusetts, "fat, filthy squawkers . . . they fought for scraps" (*MC*, 41). Ironically the Foxes are forced into a similar position at Brewer's Lagoon, despite Allie's rhetoric and vision. The three men Allie murders in Fat Boy he describes as scavengers, a strategy he uses to erase his moral responsibility for such drastic action. "Clover said, 'What's worse than dying?' 'Being turned into scavengers,' Father replied" (*MC*, 312).

Vultures hover throughout *The Mosquito Coast*, waiting for their chance to strike. Allie kills them, once gratuitously with a slingshot and later on: "He hated scavengers. . . . And, as if in revenge—but what had they done to us?—he caught them by letting them swallow baited hooks, and he plucked and roasted them. He ate them. His hunger was hatred. . . . One morning we saw that he had killed a vulture and hung it high on a tree. It stayed there, lynched, until the other birds tore it apart" (*MC*, 309). Consequently, as if the natural order of things has been upset by Allie's schemes, at the end of the book vultures pursue him: "He cried most when he saw the birds. . . . We had never seen vultures like this before" (*MC,* 364). "I'll tell you who'll inherit the world— scavenging birds" (*MC,* 366), Allie exclaims, living out his darkest visions in the moments before his death, when the family arrives at the Mosquito Coast and witnesses the vultures' scooping the turtles out of their shells to devour them. And the dark vision consumes him at last, when a solitary vulture tears out his tongue.

As John Leonard in his perceptive review pointed out, "The family is the first 'creation.' To sons, fathers are automatically gods, not only because they have violent opinions on everything . . . but especially when they test our faith by forcing us to climb trees. . . . Gods, of course, insist that their sons fail." He continues: "As a book about growing up to critical intelligence, it devastates."[16]

Allie Fox's thirteen-year-old son Charlie, the boy who idolizes his father's every move and notion and who slowly becomes aware of his madness and his self-delusions, narrates the novel, another master stroke on Theroux's part, especially to avoid repeating the often vacuous, solipsistic sermons of Maude Coffin Pratt in *Picture Palace.* The confrontation between father and son adds a further emotional and cultural resonance to the novel that transcends even its American roots and sources.

At the beginning of the book Charlie is convinced that his father is a mechanical genius, believes "that the world belonged to him and that everything he said was true" (*MC,* 11), knows that he "was the smartest man in the world" (*MC,* 16), and wants "to work, to carry the toolbox and hand him the oil can and be his slave and do anything he asked" (*MC,* 18). And yet early doubts surface in his adoration. When the family goes shopping, Charlie realizes, "Father was embarrassing in public. He took no notice of strangers" (*MC,* 43): "I was ashamed of Father, who didn't care what anyone thought. And I envied him for being so free, and hated myself for feeling ashamed" (*MC,* 33). Allie keeps his children out of school: "I felt like an old man or a freak when I saw other children" (*MC,* 41). Charlie begins to realize that his father is a disappointed man, that "something is going to happen to us" (*MC,* 51). When he hands his father's letter of resignation to Tiny Polski, Polski tells him the tale of Spider Mooney, a man who is condemned to die and who, when his father comes to visit him one last time, bites his father's ear off: "That's for makun me what I am" (*MC*, 55). About Allie, Polski adds, "I've come to see he's dangerous . . . and one of these days he's going to get you all killed" (*MC*, 55).

Once in Baltimore when Allie dares him to sit on the rock and wait for the tide to come in, Charlie eyes him differently: "He was dark, I did not know him, and he watched me like a stranger, with curiosity rather than affection. And I felt like a stranger to him. . . . I did not know him, he did not know me. I had to wait to discover who we were" (*MC*, 64). He recognizes the fact that "he needed a person there to hear his speeches" (*MC*, 95)—the novel opens, after all, with Charlie's listening to Allie's harangue—yet in his situation "I clung to him and Mother, for everything I had known that was comfortable had been taken away from me" (*MC*, 107). His belief in his father sees him through for awhile, and he decides that his father's sending him up the ship's rigging in the storm and into Fat Boy at Jeronimo "was making me a man . . . it had all been a kind of training for times like this. Father wanted me to be strong" (*MC*, 160, 181).

And yet doubts continue to erode his faith. He and the other children create the Acre as a sanctuary away from Allie's Jeronimo. Seeing Fat Boy as a symbol of his father's mind, he realizes "it had scared me" (*MC*, 170). On the journey over the mountains with the ice, his father looks "like a white corpse that had crawled out of the grave" (*MC*, 213), and Allie's lie about the Indians' being thrilled at seeing the ice he has brought them outrages his oldest son. Allie's marvels turn out to be just that, just marvels in his son's eyes, and Allie himself begins to resemble the very savages he upbraids, like "the wild man of the woods, and hollering" (*MC*, 283).

Life with father becomes "like the slow death in dreams of being trapped and trying to scream without a voice box" (*MC*, 319). Shocks of recognition disrupt his current of faith, "because we didn't count, because he was always right, always the explainer, and most of all because he ordered us to do these difficult things. He didn't want to see us succeed, he wanted to laugh at our failure" (*MC*, 328). When Allie fails to surface after diving for the shear pin, Charlie exclaims, "I had never felt safer. Father was gone. How quiet it was here. Doubt, death, grief—they had passed like the shadow of a bird's wing brushing us. . . . We were free" (*MC*, 330). The moment does not last, but the feelings do, and "when he climbed aboard, he brought all the old fear with him. I was spooked again into believing that the storm had raged across the whole world and that there was death on the coast" (*MC*, 332). Murderous thoughts enter Charlie's mind, and Charlie joins Jerry in wanting their father dead: "[Jerry] was speaking my thoughts again and making me afraid" (*MC*, 333).

Charlie's conversion is complete: "Turn your back and walk away fast—that was his motto. Invent any excuse for going. Just clear out. It had made him what he was—it was his genius. *Don't look back*" (*MC*, 343). After Allie's death, Charlie beholds a new world: "Once I had believed in Father, and the world had seemed very small and old. He was gone, and now I hardly believed in myself, and the world was limitless," and yet, "it was too early for us to feel anything except the shock of relief" (*MC*, 374). The nightmare is over.

Theroux's fondness for doubling provides the unsettling image of the scarecrow as a kind of symbol of the age-old relations between fathers and sons. The scarecrow appears like a Duppie, "your own ghost . . . they is your other self. They got bodies of they own." Back in Hatfield, Massachusetts, one dark night, feeling full "of lonesome emptiness," Charlie wakes and sneaks out into the dark to spy upon "men with torches marching at midnight across the valley fields. . . . It was a snake of flame" (*MC*, 13). The men are carrying a huge black cross and have fastened a dead man to it. It feels to Charlie "like the nightmare you watch happening to you and cannot explain. . . . But just as I saw the raised cross I remembered that I was looking for my father. The recollection and the sight came at the same instant, and I thought: That dead twisted person is my old man. . . . [It was] as if it was something I had imagined, an evil thought that had sprung out of my head. Watching it made me part of it. . . . [T]he men, these rags, foamed toward me. I picked myself up and ran for my life" (*MC*, 15). Charlie experiences both the desire to see his father dead, thus releasing himself from his subservient position, and the terror of being fatherless and, therefore, abandoned and alone. Thinking that what he has seen has been only a nightmare, he is mortified when the next day his father grins and says, "Don't tell me you've never seen a scarecrow" (*MC*, 19).

The scarecrow imagery persists in all its symbolic overtones throughout the novel. Having overheard his father's harangues and obsessions, Charlie realizes that "I had seen things that had not fitted with what I knew. Even familiar things, like that scarecrow— it had been upraised like a demon and struck terror into me" (*MC, 50*). The three men who come to Jeronimo from the Indian village to conquer it remind Charlie of "three scarecrows" (*MC, 238*), and even Allie, "the wild man of the woods," begins "looking like a live scarecrow" (*MC, 283*). Scarecrows, of course, are erected in fields to scare off the birds, to frighten the scavengers away and save the crops for harvest, but Allie cannot prevent the scavengers from swooping down on him at the end, as if Charlie's terrifying but inevitable nightmare has come true. Allie's last words sum up the frightening symbol, that strange totem representing the mystery of fathers and sons: " 'Vultures,' he said, and then the terrible sentence, 'Christ is a scarecrow!' " (*MC, 367*).

John Leonard believes that Theroux in *The Mosquito Coast* has gone on a "metaphysical binge. . . . Mr. Theroux doesn't trust his readers. He explains and underlines. . . . He won't let us guess, and he should have. He is a typical father."[17] Because of the swift pacing and inevitable plotting of the novel, Leonard's criticism seems more valid in terms of *Picture Palace* than it does of *The Mosquito Coast*. The size and scope and adventurous rush of the latter book can easily handle such images without their slowing the pace of the Honduran quest. In *The Mosquito Coast* the "metaphysical binge" fits very nicely into what Thomas R. Edwards has called "a fine entertainment, a gripping adventure story, a remarkable comic portrait of minds and cultures at cross-purposes. . . . Theroux's book . . . doesn't force us into these deep waters . . . [it] is also an impressively serious act of imagination."[18]

Theroux's first novel, *Waldo*, used the son-versus-father theme in all its one-dimensional rage and rebellion, and it is interesting that in his best novel so far, in *The Mosquito Coast*, he has returned to that vision. The vision, of course, has become far more complex and invigorating, trading as it does on well-developed symbols, the underpinnings of allegory, the journey structure of biblical quests and American fables. *The Mosquito Coast* is the supreme example so far of Theroux's fiction, revealing the artist at the top of his form. Everything in it works, delights, and appalls exactly as it should. The querulous central character, the self wrestling with an alien landscape, the extraordinary detail of jungle and nightmare and sea—Charlie's description of dawn's rising at sea has that fine descriptive and poetic edge we associate with Huckleberry Finn's description of dawn on the Mississippi—the use of doubling and paradox, the plot used not to contain inevitable collapse or shocks of recognition but to exploit them and make them seem inevitable. All these Therouxvian themes and techniques have never been better. *The Mosquito Coast* is an extraordinary novel and at this writing the apotheosis of Paul Theroux as a writer of fiction.

Chapter Seven

Theroux's Coming of Age: "Celebrating His Gift"

As Paul Theroux enters his forty-sixth year, he can certainly survey his life and his art from the pinnacle of his career. In 1982 he achieved his most celebrated and accomplished novel so far, *The Mosquito Coast*. In 1984 he was inducted into the American Academy and Institute of Arts and Letters, and in 1985 he changed publishers and signed a million-dollar deal for a new novel and a new travel book. In 1985 two films were made from his books, *The Mosquito Coast* and *Half Moon Street* (1984), the first films made from his work since *Saint Jack,* even though producers had purchased the rights to several of them. Nineteen eighty-five also saw the publication of *Sunrise with Seamonsters: Travels and Discoveries,* a collection of his essays and articles from 1964 to 1984, one more indication that he had arrived as a celebrated recognized author. Finally the *New Yorker* described *The Imperial Way,* though with only thirty pages of text, as "informative and colorful."[1]

Two short novels, "Doctor Slaughter" and "Doctor DeMarr," appeared under the title, *Half Moon Street,* Theroux's longest work of fiction since *The Mosquito Coast,* excluding the collection of short stories, *The London Embassy* (1983). In what Susan Lardner has described as Theroux's "opportunity to revel in double imagery"[2] and Christopher Lehmann-Haupt in the *New York Times* as "tricky, dazzling performances,"[3] Theroux has produced two carefully crafted tales built upon duplicity and double identities. The first, "Doctor Slaughter," focuses on the perceptions of a research fellow and student of the politics of the Persian Gulf and part-time prostitute, involving the intricacies of leading a double life and the unexpected results of her own self-delusions. "Doctor DeMarr" involves twins and what can happen when one twin takes over the identity of his identical twin brother after his death, uncertain of what the consequences will be. "In true Jekyll and Hyde tradition,"[4] notes Alice

McDermott, Theroux explores the ramifications of doubleness in all its ongoing complexities.

Lauren Slaughter, in character a close cousin to Heather Monkhouse in *Girls at Play* and Gretchen in the story "Fury" in *The London Embassy*, has come to a wintry and dreary London to write a paper on "Recycling Oil Revenue" at the Hemisphere Institute of International Studies. In her worldly innocence she considers herself to be special, stylish, and original and believes "that she could have anything she wanted."[5] She places her faith in sex and its immediate rewards: "I'm the sort of healthy open-minded girl that people used to call a nymphomaniac" (*DS*, 107). Such an innocent faith in the good body, the vegetarian diet, easy sex, and her own powers as a woman, reveals a certain mindlessness and self-centeredness that will lead to the "ravishing witch['s]" (*DS*, 59) being burned at the stake.

The Jasmine Agency, which employs her, sets her up with an Arab clientele, which leads to several sexual adventures. One Arab keeps her in a flat on Half Moon Street in Mayfair, a fashionable area in London. Later on she becomes involved with Lord Bulbeck, who is involved in some mysterious Mideast negotiations. One day a mysterious and unresponsive character, who carries a metal valise with him, turns up at her Mayfair flat. He trains a camera out the window at the Naval and Military Club across the street and just before dawn spirits her away in his car out into the country. She's convinced he will attempt to kill her and at her first opportunity flees, returning to her flat to find that everything is gone.

Lauren later learns from the mysterious mastermind of the plot that she was the bait for men he wanted to spy on, having bugged the apartment on Half Moon Street. "London is full of people like you," he tells her. "The world is. That's why it is so easy for us" (*DS*, 142). At the airport in France on her way back to the States, Lauren discovers "the same simple picture on the front page" of every newspaper; "the fallen man not only had a face but an expression—surprise, anguish, and his eyes were whitened with fear" (*DS*, 143). The murdered man is Lord Bulbeck.

The double life Lauren thinks she is leading, between the Institute by day and the Agency by night, turns out to be another one entirely. At first it intrigues her: "She was two people, and it worked so well she had at times glimpses of a third—the person she believed in and trusted" (*DS*, 97). But as the tables are turned, she recognizes only her total isolation, bereft of any identity whatsoever: "the calculated frolic of a double life that had granted her a kind of power, she now saw as a sickening weakness, a feeble plotting to serve a bad habit" (*DS*, 135). The American innocent, full of her own charms, her "body-confidence," and her "egotistical sublime" riding on motion and money and sexual power, fails to recognize the true danger of her own duplicities and is left an accomplice to assassination, an exile wandering homeward with full knowledge of her complicity and lethal cooperation.

In "Doctor DeMarr" Theroux doubles his doubles. When George DeMarr returns suddenly out of nowhere and turns up on the door-step of the family house, where Gerald has been living alone for years, he suddenly dies, and Gerald assumes his professional role as a doctor in Boston. Unfortunately, George is not a real doctor and has made his money dispensing drugs to addicts, leading his own double life. The upshot results in Gerald's being killed by the very people who murdered George to begin with, a fitting end for a deadly double game: "in George's shoes he saw that George had been right. They only had one life, and it meant one thing—the same life, the same death."[6]

Both Gerald and George hate being twins; "it made them ene-mies" (*DD*, 148). Gerald feels "that as a twin he had been buried alive" (*DD*, 149); he despises the fact that each is "the ghost of the other—a sort of maddening mimicry . . . a nation of two" (*DD*, 151), chained together. Gerald sees George as "a diseased and dis-figuring part of himself" (*DD*, 165).

The DeMarrs' ineffectual parents hover in the background, as parents tend to do in Theroux's fiction. Old Mr. DeMarr "was a salesman in a men's clothing store. . . . The jokes revealed his sadness and his sentimentality" (*DD*, 150). Theroux's father had been a salesman too. The DeMarrs lived in "a town and a neigh-borhood of Boston," which suggests Theroux's own Medford. The old man dies, "that dapper man who hid himself in his clothes; that puppeteer, that sadist" (*DD*, 155). Gerald experiences a re-curring nightmare in which his mother "drew a gun from out of her oversize coat and shot Gerald in the chest. . . . It was a toy pistol . . . and yet the woman's face had terrified him" (*DD*, 201). Dark dreams can also double and shatter a life already doubled and redoubled.

Half Moon Street is more clever than deep, and yet it does emphasize Theroux's continuing fascination with double lives, dark duplicities, and sudden double shifts in the structure of plots. The characters may be no more "than figures in an adult cartoon"[7] and certainly, as Christopher Lehmann-Haupt suggests, "the stories are not as ambitious as his last novel, *The Mosquito Coast* (1982), which in its scope and depth represented a climax in Mr. Theroux's multiform development."[8]

Lehmann-Haupt goes on "to consider how the two fictions reflect Mr. Theroux's career as a writer and his preoccupation with identity and alienation."[9] Lauren Slaughter and Gerald DeMarr suffer from both a lack of identity and a sense of social alienation; each tries to redeem herself or himself by living other lives. Each fails miserably in the attempt and is either involved with murder or is murdered. Stepping outside their narrow lives and capabilities proves fatal to them both. And each cannot write, as Lehmann-Haupt suggests. Posing as his brother, the doctor, Gerald cannot write prescriptions; Lauren cannot produce her paper. In "Doctor Slaughter" Theroux writes, "Writing was so hard. It was not just setting down your thoughts or putting those clippings into a narrative, but more like learning how to think and then teaching yourself to write. It was not just hard—it was impossible for her" (*DS,* 112). It is obviously not impossible for Paul Theroux, and perhaps as Lehmann-Haupt concludes, Theroux "can soar and he can dig. He can go anywhere he wants in the world and take his talent with him. For him there is no exile or loss of identity. In *Half Moon Street* he observes what happens to those who lack his ability. But he's also celebrating his gift."[10]

O-Zone

O-Zone, published in the late summer of 1986, is Theroux's first big novel for his new publishers, G. P. Putnam's Sons. In it he meticulously conjures up a futuristic United States in which major cities are sealed off from the rest of the country, and aliens walk the unclosed, predatory wildernesses outside. This vision first surfaces in Theroux's visit to Belfast in *The Kingdom By The Sea:* "inside the Control Zone life was fairly peaceful and the buildings generally undamaged. . . . It was conceivable that this system would in time be adapted to cities that were otherwise uncontrollable. . . . Ulster suggested to me the likely eventuality of sealed cities in the future" (*KS,* 235).

In *O-Zone* Theroux plays the perfect tour guide, showing his readers his futuristic realm. Rotors and security guards roar through the skies. The latest fashions include animal masks and naked bodies painted as savages. People check in to contact clinics for good sex, wear lunar suits on patrol, drug themselves on coma couches, and carry IDs. Godseye, a vigilant group of cowardly bullies, terrorizes and kills any aliens it comes across for the sheer pleasure of wasting them. Pilgrims have formed a space cult: "They've made a sort of scientific religion out of the space program—they're rocket people."[11] And everyone in the sealed cities, especially in New York, fears the aliens, the Trolls, the Skells, the Diggers, outlaw creatures whom they suspect of cannibalism and disease. Theroux complements this world with marvelous descriptions of wasted areas, urban slums, the green wilderness beyond the sealed cities, the forests, plains, and rivers, and California after a great earthquake. All of it is close enough to our own experience to make us shiver with recognition.

But the problem with *O-Zone* is that Theroux, the traveler, has taken over Theroux, the teller of tales. The skeletal plot and cartoonlike characters are overwhelmed by acres of speculation, explanation, and recapitulation, as if Theroux were so taken by his future realm, he ignored narrative in favor of description. Pounds of interpretation and description outweigh the ounce of plot, and in its garrulous, repetitive manner *O-Zone* reminds one of Maude Coffin Pratt's bloated babblings, of an intellect operating in a vacuum. "It was like hearing an echo but missing the original sound that caused it" (*OZ,* 302), Theroux writes and in effect summarizes the problems with this sprawling novel.

A group of Owners from New York City decide to spend their New Year's Eve in the O-Zone, a dangerous, off-limits area in Missouri that has been devastated by nuclear waste. While there they shoot two aliens. Later Hooper Allbright, a billionaire mail-order executive, the brother of Hardy Allbright, the billionaire engineer at Asfalt, sees on a videotape of the visit a beautiful young girl. He wants her. He returns to O-Zone with Fisher, the quacking-adolescent, computer-wizard, stepson of brother Hardy (who has been sent by Hardy to get the layout of the land for a huge project involving a thermal mountain and tons of asphalt), steals the girl, Bligh, and Fisher is kidnapped by Mr. Blue and his fellow aliens. Hooper gets fifteen-year-old Bligh. Blue gets fifteen-year-old Fisher.

The plot lumbers toward swapping Bligh for Fisher, although Hooper has fallen in love with Bligh, who has fallen in love with New York, and Fisher has grown into manhood alongside Mr. Blue by testing himself in the wilderness. The confrontation comes, a Godseye rotor is blown out of the sky just in time, Fisher decides to stay with Blue . . . "He had the wealth of an Owner and the strength of an alien" (*OZ,* 470)—and Bligh decides to stay with Hooper. All have been changed by their experiences. Old categories of alien and owner have collapsed. And Moura Allbright, Hardy's wife and Fisher's mother, finds true love after a long search in devastated California with the man who impregnated her with Fisher at a contact clinic years ago.

As characters, Hooper and Hardy are interchangeable, though the former is more hopeful and the latter more hard-headed. The Murdicks, friends of the Allbrights, fill their roles in the plot like stereotypes in a television screenplay: Willis the coward loves Godseye, the vigilante murderers, while his wife, Holly, looks "roasted" as a sex-starved housewife, eager for more contact at the clinic. They all seem sketches, mere ghostly presences within the greater reality of Theroux's futuristic realm.

Allegory powers the lumpen narrative somewhat, but too much of it sinks the feeble action. Fisher learns that too much technology isolates man from his environment and imprisons him. Aliens are human after all, tough survivors and not merely savage bogeymen. The Midwest is painted as some childhood repository of nostalgic habit, filled with good folk washing their cars, staging wedding receptions, and cutting the grass, not peopled with evil creatures on the prowl, as envisioned by sealed-off New Yorkers. And O-Zone passes in perspective from radioactive wilderness to challenging Eden to America's last great hope: "People dreamed about it and used it as a backdrop for their fantasies. . . . It was an area of darkness in most people's consciousness . . . [it] was now the last great chance in America . . . it was a condition and it was probably eternal, and it was everywhere. O-Zone was the world" (*OZ,* 326, 378-39, 346, 510). In such a world all action and narrative are swallowed up.

We've been to such empty spaces before in Theroux, to Cape Wrath and Patagonia, to Africa and the Honduran jungle, spaces that conjure up a nameless dread, that force the self to confront its own death and the true, often-terrible "Otherness" of the world.

"Mr. Theroux . . . has an . . . intense faith in the redemption of empty spaces," Susan Fromberg Schaeffer writes in reviewing *O-Zone* for the *New York Times*. True, but that possible redemption has always carried with it darker intimations and a kind of nihilistic *frission* of the spirit. In *O-Zone*, however, emptiness is all so much so that plot and character have been sabotaged if not nearly abandoned, and a great speculative vacuum threatens to obliterate the whole of Theroux's carefully conjured-up future. The novel finally is, as Schaeffer suggests, "a popcorn apocalypse . . . rattl[ing] at us like a badly made plastic skull,"[12] an emptiness stretched to fill a void it cannot fill.

Conclusion

In January 1986 Theroux wrote, "It wouldn't worry me if I stopped writing. I hate the thought of being housebound. I have no interest in 'society.' I am fairly interested in movies, and am writing a script [of the Mexican novel *Las muertas*] for the British director, Nicholas Roeg. But in fact that's another way of getting out of the house. If I am spared by the Almighty to write another travel book I would like to take a long trip through either China or Africa."[13] He also added, "I think it is a fatal mistake for a writer to have a great opinion of himself. I also think it's wrong for a writer to shut himself away from the world. But I do think that the very nature of writing keeps the writer from enjoying the pleasures of the earth as he should. The example I will offer is that I have a far better time traveling when I am not writing about it, and it would not bother me now to abandon writing and simply go to ground. 'He now runs a vineyard in Mexico,' would be a nice epitaph." And he is delighted "that nearly all my books are published as Penguin paperbacks—because when I was in Africa, even the local store in town got the latest Penguins (about 6 months late). It means my books travel to distant places and that everyone with a few rupees has a chance to read them."[14]

The critical response to Theroux as a writer has solidified over the years. Both *Newsweek* and the *New York Times,* in reviewing *Sunrise with Seamonsters,* have described him as "the professional man of letters,"[15] as "a distinguished member of that severely endangered species, the American man of letters."[16] Each recognizes as well the distinct voice of Theroux's fictions and other writings: "Though invariably shrewd, energetic, witty and skeptical," writes Gene Lyons, "he can also be pigheaded, obtuse, often egotistical and sometimes pompous . . . [but he] is never dull [and writes] with the unsparing eye of a seasoned traveler."[17] Michiko Kakutani finds Theroux's point of view "detached and observant—by turns amused, appalled and fascinated by the oddities and incongruities of the country—or city—he happens to be visiting. . . . Perhaps, in the end, what makes Mr. Theroux most persuasive as a writer is simply his willingness to put himself on the line, to monitor his own emotions and give us a report."[18]

Such descriptions of Theroux's voice echo Robert Towers who finds Theroux "acerbic, bookish, deadpan, observant, bibulous. . . . He can be cranky. . . . Theroux has the courage of his national prejudices. . . . The author's deadpan narrative manner can usually be counted on to keep his indignation under control."[19] All would agree with the *Times* reviewer who describes the portrait of Theroux in *Sunrise with Seamonsters* as "his coming of age as a writer and a man."[20]

And Susan Lardner in her *New Yorker* piece has nicely summed up the themes and techniques of his work: his interest in "the conflict of ideals and illusions," his "general idea of the secret sharer," which appears again and again in his tales, and his "belief in the continuing strangeness of the world. . . . Irony is his natural style." In conclusion, "Theroux operates, with nineteenth-century aplomb, as a kind of secret agent, transmitting messages from unsettled and godforsaken outposts, exciting the reader's curiosity with the vigor of his own."[21]

Theroux is, indeed, a traditional teller of tales, in that his carefully structured plots and realistic experiences do not reflect modernist texts, like Joyce, Proust, or Faulkner, nor do his well-rounded characters compare to the stick figures and cartoon creatures who perform according to some apocalyptic vision or ideology, as in the "post-modernist" novels of a Kurt Vonnegut or Thomas Pynchon. For Theroux, fiction relies on mimesis, on its similarities to and looking like life itself. It does not emphasize artifice, the self-conscious posturings and scramblings of more experimental fictionists, nor the linguistic puzzles of a John Hawkes or Donald Barthelme. The fictional tricks are there—the doublings, the images, the language—but they are always embedded in a realistic tale in a realistic landscape.

Within the realistic framework of his fiction, however, Theroux
does construct a kind of double-edged romanticism that more than
likely parallels America's own cultural contradictions between promise—the "American Dream"—and the reality of people's lives, what
John Kenny Crane describes as "some law of decay which seems
virtually irresistible and therefore terribly disillusioning" in that
doomed romantic way of much American literature.[22] In focusing
on the self in his fictions, on some querulous soul at the center of
most of his novels and many of the short stories, Theroux would
probably agree with Jerome J. McGann that "consciousness . . .
can set one free of the ruins of history and culture,"[23] a view that
many of his characters, for better or worse, try to believe in.

Theroux recognizes what many romantic poets have long recognized, "that there is no place of refuge, not in desire, not in the
mind, not in imagination. Man is in love and loves what vanishes,
and this includes—finally, tragically—even his necessary angels."[24]
His eye for historical and physical detail undermines his characters'
faith in their hopes for self-renewal and ultimate rewards. He views
history in images of decay, disruption, and death, not in terms of
mythic rebirth and renewal. The emblematic encounter in his fiction
occurs between these polarities: the historical present and the mythic
future based on some fantastic, mythic past. And yet Jack Fiori,
Calvin Mullet, Valentine Hood, and Waldo do escape, rescued by
their own consciousness or by the well-balanced plot that surrounds
them. Some, of course, do not: Alfred Munday, Allie Fox, Bettyjean
LeBow, Sam Fong, Marais, Lauren Slaughter, Gerald and George
DeMarr; and some think they escape but are left straddling uncertain
visions, like Maude Coffin Pratt.

Theroux's views seem to darken in his last novels, but he still
seems assured in believing, as he discussed in his critical book on
V. S. Naipaul, that real change takes place in the private consciousness, that public action is often muddled, uncertain, and
disastrous. In any case the Jamesian confrontation between American
innocence and a darker, more mysterious landscape underlies much
of his focus on the individual self and its consciousness, however
deluded, of itself.

"The movement of travel is merciful," Theroux has written, ex-
pressing that American sense of promise and renewal, of motion for
its own sake and of the process of discovering new places that,
however shaken, is never abandoned. True, in the modern world

America seems to be everywhere; the Third World emulates us and reflects our worst characteristics from materialistic greed to jingoistic, ideological banter. The brave new worlds may only be found in the empty plains of Patagonia, in the wild cliffs of Cape Wrath of northwestern Scotland, but the promise, however double-edged, remains intact.

In any case Theroux relies on paradox and ironic juxtapositions and coincidences to build his double-edged vision of bright symmetries and chosen opposites. As John Irwin suggests in *American Hieroglyphics,* "In imagining the structure of a bipolar opposition, we should think of it not as static but dynamic: as an equilibrium or equivalence of opposing forces on the model of electrical polarity—a balancing of mutual attraction and repulsion in which the opposites are simultaneously held together and held apart."[25] Such mutually constitutive opposites can produce, however, "a mirror image of a mirror image of a mirror image [in which] language necessarily becomes circular, sentences tend to double back on themselves, words and thoughts seem to spin with ever-increasing speed around a central void." Such may be the final problem with *Picture Palace,* the result of a process in which the self should recognize its own "inherent instability, . . . its ability to adopt any role or mask, to become anything,"[26] and tumble into the solipsistic abyss, the self-encapsulation that Theroux fears in himself when he is traveling.

Theroux in his fiction and nonfiction reveals these several American traits that place him firmly in several long traditions in American literature. Perhaps *The Mosquito Coast* is his own shock of recognition, his grappling with his American heritage on a wider scale. His American roots have always been there; he has now established them solidly once and for all.

As to the future? Yet more journeys, more messages from godforsaken outposts, more quests into the strangeness of the world and the stranger darkness of the individual soul in the latter half of the twentieth century. In mapping out such landscapes Theroux seems to be charting the possibilities for our own fragile redemption and our own frightening demise. No one could ask more from any author. And Paul Theroux, in his growth and development as a masterful writer of fiction and travel books, is doing it in style.

Notes and References

Chapter One

1. "Introduction, *Sunrise with Seamonsters* (Boston: Houghton Mifflin, 1985), 3; hereafter cited in text and below as *SS*.

2. "Discovering Dingle" (1976), in *SS,* 140.

3. Interview by James T. Yenckel, "The Wanderlust World of Paul Theroux," *Washington Post,* 30 December 1984, sec. G, p 2. as Yenckel.

4. Ibid., p. 1.

5. *The Old Patagonian Express* (Boston: Houghton Mifflin, 1979), 169; hereafter cited in text as *PE*.

6. *The Great Railway Bazaar* (New York: Ballantine Books, 1979), 248; hereafter cited in text as *RB*.

7. *V. S. Naipaul: An Introduction to His Work* (London: Andre Deutsch, 1972), 77; hereafter cited in text as *N*.

8. *Charles Ruas, Conversations with American Writers* (New York: Knopf, 1985), 246.

9. James Atlas, "The Theroux Family Arsenal," *New York Times Magazine,* 30 April 1978, p.24.

10. Ibid.

11. *Half Moon Street* (Boston: Houghton Mifflin, 1984), 149; hereafter cited in text as *HMS*.

12. Yenckel, "Wanderlust World," sec. G, p. 2.

13. Atlas, "Theroux," 24, 54.

14. Ibid., 54.

15. *Jungle Lovers* (Boston: Houghton Mifflin, 1971), 187, 188.

16. "Traveling Home: High School Reunion" (1979), in *SS,* 189, 190, 191, 193.

17. "Being A Man" (1983), in *SS,* 309.

18. Ruas, *Conversations,* 258.

19. *Waldo* (Boston: Houghton Mifflin, 1967), 192; hereafter cited in text as *W*.

20. "My Extended Family" (1977), in *SS,* 164.

21. Atlas, "Theroux," 49.

22. Ibid., 24.

23. Ibid., 49.

24. Ruas, *Conversations,* 249.

25. Atlas, "Theroux," 24, 49.

26. Ibid., 49, 24.

27. Ibid., 52.

28. Ibid.

29. Letter to the author, 25 July 1979. Cited below as Letter.

30. Atlas, "Theroux," 54.

31. "Cowardice" (1967), in *SS,* 41.

32. Interview with Robert Taylor, author and book reviewer for the *Boston Globe,* at Wheaton College, Norton, Massachusetts, 13 April 1985.

33. "The Killing of Hastings Banda" (1971), in *SS,* 67.

34. "Introducing *Jungle Lovers*" (1984), in *SS,* 329.

35. Atlas, "Theroux," 54.

36. "Scenes from a Curfew" (1966), in *SS,* 23–30.

37. *Sinning with Annie and Other Stories* (London: Hamish Hamilton, 1975), 116.

38. "*A Love-Scene After Work:* Writing in the Tropics" (1971), in *SS,* 83.

39. Ruas, *Conversations,* 247.

40. Atlas, "Theroux," 58.

41. Robert Towers, "A Certified American in a Highly English Mode," review of *The Great Railway Bazaar, New York Times Book Review,* 24 August 1975, p. 1.

42. Ruas, *Conversations,* 250.

43. Ibid., 24.

44. Letter.

45. Herbert Mitgang, "Paul Theroux Changing Publishers After 20 Years," *New York Times,* 27 August 1985.

46. Letter.

Chapter Two

1. *Picture Palace* (New York: Ballantine Books, 1978), 89.

2. *The Consul's File* (New York: Washington Square Press, 1984), 54; hereafter cited in text as *CF.*

3. Ruas, *Conversations,* 251.

4. Towers, "A Certified American," 2.

5. Susan Lardner, "Perfect Stranger," review of *Half Moon Street, New Yorker,* 7 January 1985, p. 72.

6. Ruas, *Conversations,* 253.

7. Letter to the author, 25 July 1979. Cited below as Letter.

8. W. J. Harvey, *Character and the Novel* (Ithaca: Cornell University Press, 1965).

9. Frederick R. Karl, *American Fictions, 1940–1980* (New York: Harper & Row, 1983), 520.

10. "*A Love-Scene after Work:* Writing in the Tropics" (1971), in *SS,* 89.

11. Lardner, "Stranger," 75.

12. Letter.

13. Ibid.

14. Ruas, *Conversations,* 262, 264.

15. Letter.

16. Towers, "A Certified American," 2.

17. Letter.

18. *Girls at Play* (New York: Ballantine Books, 1978), 131.

19. *The Kingdom by the Sea* (Boston: Houghton Mifflin, 1983), 277.

20. Letter.

21. Ibid.

22. Robert F. Bell, "Metamorphoses and Missing Halves: Allusions in Paul Theroux's *Picture Palace," Critique: Studies in Modern Fiction* 22, 3 (1981):17–30.

23. Lardner, "Stranger," 75.

24. Robert L. Caserio, *Plot, Story, and the Novel: From Dickens and Poe to the Modern Period* (Princeton: Princeton University Press, 1979).

25. Letter.

26. Caserio, *Plot,* 232.

27. Paul Theroux, "My Extended Family," (1977) in *SS,* 157.

28. Caserio, *Plot,* 269.

29. Letter.

30. Ruas, *Conversations,* 255, 250.

31. Interview by Yenckel, "Wanderlust World," sec. G, pp. 1–3.

32. "Cowardice" (1967) in *SS,* 47.

33. Karl, *American Fictions,* 520.

34. Towers, "A Certified American," 2.

35. Paul Gray, "Backwaters and Eccentrics," review of *The Mosquito Coast, Time,* 22 February 1982, p. 72.

36. Auberon Waugh, "Britain was Elsewhere," review of *The Kingdom by the Sea, New York Times Book Review,* 23 October 1983, p. 45.

37. Peter S. Prescott, "That Sour, Unstately Isle," review of *The Kingdom by the Sea, Newsweek,* 24 October 1983, p. 120.

38. John Skow, "Dodger," review of *The Kingdom by the Sea, Time,* 1 October 1983, p. 111.

39. Anatole Broyard, review in *New York Times,* 31 May 1984.

40. Theroux, letter to the author, 12 January 1986.

41. Caserio, *Plot,* 265, 266.

42. Lardner, "Stranger," 74.

43. Harvey, pp. 204, 208.

44. Letter to the author, 25 July 1979.

Chapter Three

1. Paul Theroux, *The Kingdom by the Sea* (Boston: Houghton Mifflin, 1983), 26; hereafter cited in text as *KS*.

2. Towers, "A Certified American," 1.

3. Sacvan Bercovitch, *The Puritan Origins of the American Self* (New Haven: Yale University Press, 1975), 63.

4. Larzer Ziff, *Puritanism in America: New Culture in a New World* (New York: Viking, 1973), 6.

5. Ruas, *Conversations,* 250.

6. Interview by Yenckel, "Wanderlust World" sec. G, pp. 1–3.

7. Bercovitch, *American Self,* 133.

8. Towers, "A Certified American," 2.

9. Eric Valli, "Life in Dolpo reflects rugged simplicity—as it has for centuries," *Smithsonian* 16, 8 (November 1985):135.

10. Letter to the author, 25 July 1979.

11. Yenckel, "Wanderlust World," sec. G, p. 3.

Chapter Four

1. Ruas, *Conversations,* 255.

2. Ibid.

3. Malcolm Cowley, quoted on the first page of *World's End and Other Stories* (New York: Washington Square Press, 1981); hereafter cited in text as *WE*.

4. Letter to the author, 25 July 1979.

5. *Sinning with Annie and Other Stories* (London: Hamish Hamilton, 1975), 177; hereafter cited in text as *SA*.

6. Ruas, *Conversations,* 259, 253.

7. Ibid., 257.

8. Ibid., 257, 258.

9. Ibid., 256.

10. Ibid., 253.

11. Ibid., 252.

12. *The Consul's File* (New York: Washington Square Press, 1984), 202; hereafter cited in text as *CF*.

13. Letter.

14. Philip Mason, *Prospero's Magic: Some Thoughts on Class and Race* (London: Oxford University Press, 1962).

15. *The London Embassy* (New York: Washington Square Press, 1984), 10; hereafter cited in text as *LE*.

Chapter Five

1. Atlas, "Theroux," 49.

2. "Author's Note" (London, 1975), in *Fong and the Indians* (London: Hamish Hamilton, 1976); hereafter cited in text as *FI*.

3. *Murder at Mount Holly* (London: Alan Ross, 1969), 94 in the MS version; hereafter cited in text as *MMH*.

4. "Introducing Jungle Lovers" (1984) in *SS,* 329; hereafter cited in text and below as *SS.*
5. *Jungle Lovers* (Boston: Houghton Mifflin, 1971), 122; hereafter cited in text as *JL.*
6. *Girls at Play* (New York: Ballantine Books, 1978), 34; hereafter cited in text as *GAP.*
7. "Tarzan is an Expatriate" (1967) in *SS,* 33.
8. Atlas, "Theroux," 54.
9. Letter to the author, 25 July 1979.
10. *The Black House* (London: Coronet Books, Hodder & Stoughton, 1976), 64; hereafter cited in text as *BH.*

Chapter Six

1. Letter to the author, 12 January 1986.
2. *Saint Jack* (New York: Penguin, 1976), 21; hereafter cited in text as *SJ.*
3. *The Family Arsenal* (New York: Washington Square Press, 1984), 18; hereafter cited in text as *FA.*
4. *Picture Palace* (New York: Ballantine Books, 1978), 100; hereafter cited in text as *PP.*
5. Robert F. Bell, "Metamorphoses and Missing Halves: Allusions in Paul Theroux's *Picture Palace,*" *Critique: Studies in Modern Fiction* 22, 3, (1981):17–30.
6. Ibid., 24.
7. Ibid., 27, 28.
8. *The Mosquito Coast* (New York: Avon, 1983), 3; hereafter cited in text as *MC.*
9. Thomas R. Edwards, "Paul Theroux's Yankee Crusoe," review of *The Mosquito Coast, New York Times Book Review,* 14 February 1982, p. 24.
10. "Being a Man," (1983) in *SS,* 309, 310.
11. Alexis de Tocqueville, *Democracy in America,* trans. Henry Reeve, ed. Phillips Bradley (New York: Random House, 1945), 2: 3 cited by John P. McWilliams, Jr., in *Hawthorne, Melville, and the American Character: A Looking-glass Business* (Cambridge: Cambridge University Press, 1984), 163.
12. McWilliams, *Hawthorne . . .,* 228, 8, 9, 9–10.
13. Ibid., 137, 10.
14. John Irwin, *American Hieroglyphics* (New Haven: Yale University Press, 1980) 286.
15. McWilliams, *Hawthorne . . .,* 20.
16. John Leonard, review of *The Mosquito Coast, New York Times,* 11 February 1982, sec. C, p. 31.

17. Ibid.

18. Edwards, "Yankee Crusoe," 24.

Chapter Seven

1. Anonymous review, *New Yorker,* 6 January 1986, p. 86.

2. Lardner, "Stranger," review of *Half Moon Street, New Yorker,* 7 January 1985, p. 75.

3. Christopher Lehmann-Haupt, review of *Half Moon Street, New York Times,* 1 October 1984, sec. C, p. 16.

4. Alice McDermott, "Ravishing Witch, Ph.D.," review of *Half Moon Street, New York Times Book Review,* 28 October 1984, p. 35.

5. "Doctor Slaughter," in *Half Moon Street* (Boston: Houghton Mifflin, 1984), 71; hereafter cited in text as *DS.*

6. "Doctor DeMarr," in *Half Moon Street,* 219; hereafter cited in text as *DD.*

7. McDermott, "Witch," 35.

8. Lehmann-Haupt review, 1 October, 1984.

9. Ibid.

10. Ibid.

11. *O-Zone* (New York: G. P. Putnam's Sons, 1986), 340; hereafter cited in text as *OZ.*

12. Susan Fromberg Schaeffer, "Nerd of Paradise," review of *O-Zone, New York Times Book Review,* 21 September 1986, pp. 12, 13.

13. Letter to the author, 12 January 1986.

14. Ibid.

15. Gene Lyons, "A Combative American Abroad," review of *Sunrise with Seamonsters, Newsweek,* 12 August 1985, pp. 66C, 66D.

16. Michiko Kakutani, review of *Sunrise with Seamonsters, New York Times,* 5 July 1985, sec. C, p. 24.

17. Lyons, "Combative American."

18. Kakutani, review of *SS,* sec. C, p. 24.

19. Towers, "A Certified American," 2.

20. Kakutani, review of *SS,* sec. C, p. 24.

21. Lardner, "Stranger," 75–76.

22. John Kenny Crane, *The Root of All Evil: The Thematic Unity in William Styron's Fiction* (Columbia, S.C.: University of South Carolina Press, 1984), 20.

23. Jerome J. McGann, *The Romantic Ideology: A Critical Investigation* (Chicago: University of Chicago Press, 1983), 91.

24. Ibid., 145.

25. Irwin, *American Hieroglyphics,* 102.

26. Ibid., 134, 320.

Selected Bibliography

PRIMARY SOURCES

1. Novels
The Black House. Boston: Houghton Mifflin, 1974. Reprint. London: Coronet Books, 1976; New York: Washington Square Press, 1984.
The Family Arsenal. Boston: Houghton Mifflin, 1976. Reprint. London: Penguin, 1977; New York: Washington Square Press, 1984.
Fong and the Indians. Boston: Houghton Mifflin, 1968. Reprint. London: Hamish Hamilton, 1976.
Girls at Play. Boston: Houghton Mifflin, 1969. Reprint. London: The Bodley Head, 1969; New York: Ballantine Books, 1978; New York: Washington Square Press, 1984.
Half Moon Street. Boston: Houghton Mifflin, 1984. *Doctor Slaughter* was published separately in England. London: Hamish Hamilton, 1984.
Jungle Lovers. Boston: Houghton Mifflin, 1971. Reprint. London: The Bodley Head, 1971.
The Mosquito Coast. Boston: Houghton Mifflin, 1982. Reprint New York: Avon, 1983.
Murder in Mount Holly. London: Alan Ross, 1969.
O-Zone. New York: G. P. Putnam's Sons, 1986.
Picture Palace. Boston: Houghton Mifflin, 1978. Reprint. New York: Ballantine Books, 1978.
Saint Jack. Boston: Houghton Mifflin, 1973. Reprint. London: The Bodley Head, 1973. New York: Penguin, 1976; New York: Washington Square Press, 1984.
Waldo. Boston: Houghton Mifflin, 1967. Reprint. London: The Bodley Head, 1968.

2. Travel Books
The Great Railway Bazaar: By Train through Asia. Boston: Houghton Mifflin, 1975. Reprint. New York: Ballantine Books, 1976.
The Imperial Way: By Rail from Peshawar to Chittagong. Boston: Houghton Mifflin, 1985.
The Kingdom By The Sea: A Journey around Great Britain. Boston: Houghton Mifflin, 1983.
The Old Patagonian Express: By Train through the Americas. Boston: Houghton Mifflin, 1979.

Patagonia Revisited. Boston: Houghton Mifflin, 1985; London: Michael
    Russell, 1985.
Sailing through China. Boston: Houghton Mifflin, 1984; London: Michael
    Russell, 1983.

3. Collections of Short Stories
The Consul's File. Boston: Houghton Mifflin, 1977. Reprint. New York:
    Ballantine Books, 1978; New York: Washington Square Press, 1984.
The London Embassy. Boston: Houghton Mifflin, 1983. Reprint. New York:
    Washington Square Press, 1984.
Sinning with Annie and Other Stories. Boston: Houghton Mifflin, 1972.
    Reprint. London: Hamish Hamilton, 1975.
World's End and Other Stories. Houghton Mifflin, 1980. Reprint. New
    York: Washington Square Press, 1981.

4. Criticism and Collections of Essays
V. S. Naipaul: An Introduction to his Work. London: Andre Deutsch, 1972.
Sunrise with Seamonsters: Travels and Discoveries. Boston: Houghton Mifflin,
    1985.

5. Children's Books
A Christmas Card. Boston: Houghton Mifflin, 1978.
London Snow: A Christmas Story. London: Michael Russell Ltd, 1979.

SECONDARY SOURCES

1. Articles, Reviews, and Interviews
Atlas, James. "The Theroux Family Arsenal." *New York Times Magazine,*
    30 April 1978, pp. 22–64. A comprehensive biographical essay on
    the Theroux family. Atlas discusses "the prolific clan of writers," the
    parents, and especially Paul's upbringing, education, and career, com-
    plete with interviews of several family members. He also concentrates
    on the eccentricities of Alexander, the second most published writer
    in the family.
Bell, Robert F. "Metamorphoses and Missing Halves: Allusions in Paul
    Theroux's *Picture Palace.*" *Critique: Studies in Modern Fiction* 22, 3
    (1981):17–30. A close look at literary allusions which refer to works
    by T. S. Eliot and Thomas Mann, particularly *The Waste Land* and
    Felix Krull. Bell shows Theroux's indebtedness to and use of doubling
    images from these authors in coming "to terms with the literary
    masters of the past. . . ."

Edwards, Thomas R. "Paul Theroux's Yankee Crusoe." Review of *The Mosquito Coast. New York Times Book Review,* 14 February 1982, pp. 1 and 24. Edwards links Theroux to fictional traditions in British Anglo-colonial literature and American literature and describes *The Mosquito Coast* as showing "a cosmopolitan expatriate novelist pondering his imaginative sources as an American writer, and the relation of those sources to the world as it now seems to be."

Lardner, Susan. "Perfect Stranger." Review of *Half Moon Street. New Yorker,* 7 January 1985, pp. 72–76. A crisp, perceptive summary of Theroux's themes and techniques as a writer in terms of his ironic style, the strangeness of the world he perceives, the complex duplicities and deceptions in that world, and the constant clash between personal ideals and self-delusions.

Ruas, Charles, *Conversations with AmericanWriters.* New York: Knopf, 1985. Pp. 244–64. An in-depth interview with Theroux in terms of his French-Canadian and New England background, his use of travel as a way of seeing, and his descriptions of America as "the Catholic Church, with a Borgia Pope." Theroux discusses his collection of short stories, *World's End,* in particular "World's End," "The Greenest Island," and "Zombies."

Towers, Robert. "A Certified American in a Highly English Mode." Review of *The Great Railway Bazaar. New York Times Book Review.* 24 August 1975, pp. 1–2. The first major review of Theroux's work. Towers concentrates on Theroux as a British writer in terms of "his comic celebration of seediness," his love of eccentric travel books, his use of the Gothic tradition in his fiction, and his look at "the anomalies of post-imperial life" in the defunct British Empire. He also describes Theroux's persona in his first travel book as "acerbic, bookish, deadpan, observant, bibulous, and rather passive. . . . "

Yenckel, James T. "The Wanderlust World of Paul Theroux." *Washington Post,* 30 December 1984. sec. G, pp. 1–3. The interview focuses on the importance of travel to Theroux as a writer and artist in terms of his persistent delight in it, his exploration of the world at large, and the importance and worth of travel literature as literature.

Index

813.54
T 412
120 045